THE SECRET OF DRUMSHEE CASTLE

Drumshee Timeline Series
Book 3

Praise for the Drumshee Timeline Series:

'... as a way of bringing a way of life long past
vividly alive ... this cannot be beaten.'
Books Ireland

'A world full of secrets, hidden treasures and adventures.'
Magpie

'An excellent way to introduce history to
the eight plus age group.'
Dublin Echo

OTHER TITLES BY CORA HARRISON

Nuala & her Secret Wolf
Drumshee Timeline Series Book 1

The Secret of the Seven Crosses
Drumshee Timeline Series Book 2

The Secret of 1798
Drumshee Timeline Series Book 4

The Famine Secret
Drumshee Timeline Series Book 5

Titanic — Voyage from Drumshee
Drumshee Timeline Series Book 6

millennium@drumshee
Drumshee Timeline Series Book 7

The Drumshee Rebels
Drumshee Timeline Series Book 8

The Viking at Drumshee
Drumshee Timeline Series Book 9

Cora Harrison taught primary-school children in England for twenty-five years before moving to a small farm in Kilfenora, Co. Clare. The farm includes an Iron Age fort, with the remains of a small castle inside it, and the mysterious atmosphere of this ancient place gave Cora the idea for a series of historical novels tracing the survival of the ringfort through the centuries. *The Secret of Drumshee Castle* follows *Nuala & her Secret Wolf* and *The Secret ofThe Seven Crosses* in the Drumshee Timeline Series.

THE SECRET OF DRUMSHEE CASTLE

Drumshee Timeline Series
Book 3

Cora Harrison

WOLFHOUND PRESS
Celebrating 25 *Years*

Reprinted 2000
First published 1998 by
WOLFHOUND PRESS Ltd
68 Mountjoy Square
Dublin 1

©1998 Cora Harrison
Illustrations © Wolfhound Press

 The Arts Council
An Chomhairle Ealaíon
Wolfhound Press receives financial assistance from The Arts Council/An Chomhairle Ealaíon, Dublin, Ireland.

British Library Cataloguing in Publication Data
A catalogue record for this book is available from the British Library.

ISBN 0-86327-632-6

10 9 8 7 6 5 4 3 2

Typesetting: Wolfhound Press
Cover illustration: Peter Gibson
Text illustrations: Orla Roche
Cover design: Sally Mills-Westley
Printed and bound by The Guernsey Press Co Ltd, Guernsey, Channel Islands

CHAPTER ONE

Grace Barry climbed the grey stone steps leading up to the three-hundred-year-old castle of Drumshee. The steps were high and she was small for her age, so she climbed slowly, hating the long, stiff, tight-waisted dress which clung around her legs. She wished she was wearing her old petticoat. She wished she was back in the only real home she had known in all her seven years — her foster-home, the little cottage beside Lough Fergus. Above all, she wished she was with Bridget. Bridget was her foster-mother, soft, warm and kind. If only she could come here with me, thought Grace, I wouldn't mind this place so much.

She stood at the top of the steps and looked all around her. She found it hard to understand that all this was now hers. The huge stone castle, the big circular enclosure with the high wall around it, the massive iron gates, the stables; and beyond, the fields, the River Fergus, the woods, the little hills and the peat bogs. What was it that her foster-brother Enda had said? Grace tried to remember the number he had used; it did not mean much to her, but in her mind she could still hear his voice vibrating with excitement.

'Four thousand acres, Grace!' he had said. 'You're the mistress of four thousand acres and a castle too. You're the richest person in the neighbourhood.'

She did not care. She did not even care that her

father and mother had died only a week before; she had never really known them, and she did not know whether she would have loved them if they were still alive. What she did know was that she hated her father's sister, Mary Fitzgerald, and Mary's husband John Fitzgerald. They had been staying in the castle when Grace's father and mother had died, and they had stayed on to be her guardians. She hated them more than anyone she had known in her life.

Sighing deeply, Grace pushed open the heavy oak door, stepped inside, and opened the door to the Great Hall.

The Great Hall at Drumshee was magnificent: the stone ceiling was high and arched, and the walls were covered with woven tapestries and painted leather hangings. Down the middle of the room ran a huge oak table, and at the far side a fire burned in the great fireplace. Beside the fire sat a woman — a middle-aged woman with icy blue eyes, iron-grey hair and long hands with talon-like nails.

Grace went towards her aunt, slowly and reluctantly, her feet dragging through the rushes which covered the flagstoned floor.

'Where have you been?' asked the harsh voice from the fireside.

Grace did not reply. She was desperately summoning up her courage to beg, to plead, to promise anything if she could only get away from all this cold splendour and back to the cosy little cottage by Lough Fergus. She struggled to find the right words, but in the end she could only say: 'I want to go home, Aunt.'

'This is your home,' said her aunt. 'Your father had no son, no other relation — except me, of course — so this is yours now.'

A wave of anger swept over Grace. 'I want to go home!' she yelled, deliberately losing her temper. This usually worked well with Bridget; but Mary Fitzgerald rose from her place by the fire and, towering over Grace, slapped her across the face with all her strength.

Grace gasped. The blow had almost knocked her off her feet, and she clung to the corner of the table. For a moment she felt sick and giddy; then a torrent of rage flooded through her.

'You horrible woman!' she screamed. 'I hate you! I hate you! I'm not going to stay here. I'm going straight back to Bridget!'

'You will never see Bridget again,' said Mary Fitzgerald venomously. 'You had better mind your manners, or you will be whipped.'

But Grace did not care. She was carried away by the worst temper tantrum of her life.

'I hate you, I hate you, I hate you!' she cried. Then, seeing that her aunt did not really care, she added spitefully: 'They were talking about you both in the kitchen last night, and they said that Mary Fitzgerald would murder her own mother for a fistful of silver and that John Fitzgerald was a wastrel and a gambler.'

There was silence for a moment. Grace began to grow frightened. There was a look in Mary Fitzgerald's eyes which she had never seen before. The angry red drained out of Grace's face, and it became as white as her aunt's.

The two stared at each other for a few long minutes;

and then Grace gave a little whimper of fear. The sound broke the tension which held them both. Grace's aunt seized the ivory-topped cane which stood by the fireplace and began beating her with a cold ferocity which knew no mercy. Grace fought and screamed and kicked, but it was no use. The more she fought, the more she was beaten, until finally she lay limp on the floor.

She barely felt her aunt drag her to the small cold bedroom at the top of the castle. She was flung onto the bed; then she heard the key turn in the lock and her aunt's footsteps going down the spiral staircase. Grace pulled the rough bedcovers over her head, curled up like a small wounded animal, and fell asleep.

It was dark when she woke up. For a moment she did not know where she was; then the pain of her stiffening bruises and the icy chill of the air around her reminded her.

She heard the key in the door turn cautiously. She sat up, stiff with fear that her aunt had come back to beat her again, but the face in the candlelight was not Mary Fitzgerald's. It was Deirdre, the cook, and she was carrying a plate of something which smelt good. Grace realised that she was very hungry. It must be quite late, she thought.

'I've brought you a sup of soup, my love,' whispered the cook. 'Did she hurt you bad?'

Grace nodded, the tears starting to her eyes. She resolutely blinked them back. I won't think of my aunt now, she thought. I'll think about her later. Now I'll just enjoy the soup and the bread, and go back to sleep, and tomorrow I'll think of some way to get back to Bridget's cottage.

'How many miles is it to Lough Fergus?' she asked. 'How long would it take me to walk it, Deirdre?'

'Oh, don't be thinking like that,' said Deirdre, alarmed. 'She'll kill you if you do anything like that. She's sent a message over to Bridget, to tell her that she mustn't come to the castle and you mustn't see her again.'

The tears welled up again in Grace's eyes. She shook her head angrily and blinked them away.

'What am I going to do, then?' she said petulantly. 'I must see Bridget and Enda. I'll die anyway if I live in this place. I hate it. It's so cold in this room.'

Deirdre looked at her uncomfortably. 'It's the worst room in the place that she's given you,' she said, feeling the bedcovers with a worried air. 'It's terribly damp. I'll see if we can get a brazier in here.'

'What's a brazier?' asked Grace. She did not really care, but it was nice to have Deirdre in there talking to her and being kind to her.

'A brazier is a sort of iron basket that you stand on the floor. You put in some sods of turf and light them, and it warms the room.'

'Bridget's cottage is always warm,' said Grace sadly. 'She always keeps a fire burning, winter and summer. I helped Enda and Bridget to get the turf last year. We brought it back on the cart and piled it up against the wall of the house.' She clenched her hands to stop the tears coming back, and quickly swallowed some soup to ease the ache in her throat.

'I'll tell you what you can do,' said Deirdre. 'You finish up that soup and then I'll sneak you down to the kitchen. I'll lock the door behind us. She won't bother looking in at you. She and her husband and that new governess they've got for you are all having dinner. You come down and have a good warm-up by the kitchen fire.'

'Is she all right?' whispered Joe, the stableman, as Grace tiptoed into the kitchen, sheltering behind Deirdre's bulk.

'She's half killed,' Deirdre whispered back. 'You wouldn't treat a horse the way that woman treated the poor child.'

Joe said nothing, but he lifted Grace up in his arms and sat her on his knee. He took off the stiff leather shoes which she hated so much and warmed her cold feet at the fire. 'What happened?' he said after a while. 'Why did she beat you like that?'

'I wanted to go back to Bridget and live with her again,' said Grace. She did not like to tell him that she had repeated the conversation between himself and Deirdre, and that that was what had thrown Mary Fitzgerald into such a passion. She snuggled in against Joe's shoulder. She knew him well. He had always been the one who brought messages and presents from the castle to her; and during the last week, since she had come to the castle, her only comfort had been helping him in the stables. Grace loved horses; her foster-brother Enda had taught her to ride almost as soon as she could walk.

'I'll tell you what,' advised Joe. 'Don't say another word about Bridget. Let *her* think you've forgotten Bridget. Then, when she and her husband go off for the day to Galway or out driving, you can easily slip across. It's only about an hour's walk.'

Grace nodded. Her head was drooping and her

eyelids kept falling down.

She slept warmly and securely in Joe's arms, but from time to time words drifted in to her through the thick cloud of sleepiness: money — inheritance — murder — danger for the child — danger, danger, danger ...

She was being shaken awake by Deirdre.

'Grace, wake up. We must get you back to your bed. They've finished their dinner. Come on, I'll take you up.'

Suddenly wide awake and carrying her shoes in her hand, Grace followed Deirdre out of the kitchen and into the little room beside the Great Hall, at the bottom of the staircase. Deirdre put her finger to her lips and inclined her ear towards the door, then gave a satisfied nod. John Fitzgerald's hoarse, rasping voice could be heard plainly from within, followed by the flat, monotonous tones of his wife. Deirdre placed one foot on the first stair; but suddenly they heard a door being pushed open, somewhere above them, and a flicker of candlelight lit up the dark walls.

'Deirdre,' said the shrill voice of Joan Butler, Grace's new governess. 'Deirdre, the warming pan in my bed is almost cold. Take it down to the kitchen and put some hot sods in it.'

Grace slipped like a little shadow behind the velvet curtain which screened the door to the Great Hall from draughts. She would be quite hidden there, and she could hear her aunt and uncle plainly; if there was any danger of them coming to the door, she would be able to slip quickly down to the kitchen again.

She could hear Deirdre pounding up the stairs to collect the warming pan. It would take her a while: she would have to take the burnt sods out of the great brass dish, carefully select new ones, make sure that they were smouldering but not burning, and then take the pan back up to the governess. All in all, Grace reckoned that it would take Deirdre a good five minutes to attend to the governess, so out of boredom she began to listen to her aunt and uncle's conversation.

'It's a pity the child didn't go too,' said her uncle's voice.

Go? thought Grace. Go where?

She was puzzled, but her aunt's next words drove the puzzle out of her head.

'Don't worry,' Mary Fitzgerald said, softly but so distinctly that the sound came clearly to the listening ears of the child behind the door. 'Don't worry. After all, we are her guardians until she's eighteen. We will have complete control over all her money until then — and who knows what might happen during the next eleven years? She may look pink-cheeked and plump now, but children die easily. And when she does, the castle and lands of Drumshee will all be mine.'

CHAPTER TWO

The next day, early in the morning, Grace settled down to work with Joan Butler the governess.

Grace had had a terrible shock. Her whole body ached from the beating, and she knew that she would never be able to get her own way with her aunt. Her mind was still filled with hatred for Mary Fitzgerald, but she knew she would have to go carefully, to be cunning, or she might never see Bridget and Enda again.

Her governess found her unlettered but quick and eager to learn — a silent, obedient child, thought Joan Butler. She would give no trouble. Lesson followed lesson: reading, writing, sewing, carefully picking out tunes on the yellow keys of the virginal in the corner of the library. Every time there was a step on the stone stairs outside, Grace stiffened; but the library was at the very top of the castle and Mary Fitzgerald did not bother to climb all those stairs.

In the middle of the afternoon, while Grace was obediently trying to hobble through the steps of a dance, in spite of her stiff legs, there was a noise on the gravel outside. A day earlier, Grace would have rushed to the window to see what was happening; but now she hesitated and looked at her governess. Joan smiled at her.

'Go and have a look,' she said kindly. 'I think it's your uncle and aunt on their way to Galway for a few days.'

Grace crossed the room and stood looking out. The carriage with its four grey horses was drawn up in front of the castle, and Mary Fitzgerald, followed by her husband, was just about to get in.

Mary's eye was caught by the movement at the window high above her, and she looked up. Even from this distance, Grace could see that her aunt's face was full of malevolence. Her heart sank. She remembered what she had heard the night before, and suddenly a rush of resolve came to her.

I'm not going to die, she said to herself firmly. No one is going to put me in a box in the ground. I'm going to stay alive, and I'm going to find some way to punish that woman for what she's done to me.

Slowly she turned away from the window and went back to her governess. I hope there aren't too many more lessons, she thought. My head is beginning to ache.

Joan smiled at her.

'You're looking rather pale,' she said. 'I think we'll finish for today. You've done very well. You can go for a little walk, or you can lie down on your bed. I have some sewing to do for your aunt.'

Outside the door, Grace hesitated. She did feel tired, but she hated the thought of going into her cold, damp bedroom. Perhaps she would go out to the stables and see if Joe was there and needed some help with the horses.

Joe was in front of the castle, carefully raking the gravel to hide the traces of the carriage wheels.

'You're looking a little better this afternoon,' he said kindly. 'You go into the stables now and you'll find a nice surprise.'

Perhaps there's a new horse, thought Grace. She went into the stable — and there was Enda, her foster-brother, sitting on a bale of straw.

After Bridget, Enda was the person Grace loved best in the world. She had been only a tiny baby when she came to Bridget's house to be fostered; and from that day, Enda, five years older than Grace, had looked after and played with and cared for the little girl from the castle. As Grace looked at his smooth brown face with the gentle dark eyes, so like his mother's, all her self-control left her and she started to cry. She cried so much that Enda, after some vain attempts to stop her, ran out to fetch Joe, and Joe got Deirdre .

'Don't cry now, little darling,' said Deirdre. 'Look, I've brought you some cake. Go on, have a little bite. Go on now, or I'll give it to the horse! Look at him. He can smell it. Look at him leaning out of his box and opening his big mouth. Go on, look at his big yellow teeth!'

Grace wiped her eyes and looked, and a watery smile came over her face. She brushed back her curls and took a bite of the cake. She found it hard to swallow, but once she had managed to get a mouthful down, she began to feel a little better.

'I'll save a bit for Sultan,' she said.

'No, don't you save any,' scolded Deirdre. 'Joe, you go inside and bring out a couple more of these cakes. The lad can have one as well.'

'My mother would like to see Grace,' said Enda, when Joe had come back with the cakes.

Grace said nothing. Her heart was thumping, but she carried on feeding Sultan, the big black horse, who had been her father's hunting stallion.

'Better not,' said Joe hastily. 'You know what *she* said.'

Grace knew that when Joe said '*she*' in that tone, he was talking about her aunt. She went on putting little bits of cake into Sultan's mouth.

'She's waiting down in the river meadows, just below the castle,' went on Enda. 'She's hiding in the blackthorn bushes there. She won't let anyone see her, but she wants to make sure that Grace is all right.'

Grace could keep silent no longer. 'Oh, please let me go! My governess said I could go for a walk. No one will see me with her. I'll stay hidden in the bushes. I want to see Bridget!'

Deirdre thought for a moment. 'It can't do any harm,' she said eventually to Joe. 'Enda had better go away first, so they aren't seen together, and then I'll walk down with the child myself. A bit of exercise will do me good. I'm getting too fat.'

'I'd better take off these shoes,' said Grace eagerly. 'They'll only get wet and muddy in the fields.'

'That's a good idea,' said Joe heartily. 'The child is quite right, Deirdre; she's used to going barefoot, and there will be trouble if the leather shoes are spoiled.'

'I think I should take off this dress, too,' said Grace, eagerly seizing the opportunity. 'I've got my old petticoat in the chest in my room. I'll just run upstairs and change. No one will see me. My governess is in her room and her window looks west.'

Deirdre smiled. 'You'll be the death of me,' she said resignedly, 'but I suppose it would be a pity if that lovely dress got torn on the blackthorn bushes.'

Lovely dress, indeed, thought Grace as she sped up the stone stairs, her bruises forgotten in the excitement of seeing Bridget again. Lovely dress! It's the most horrible thing I've ever worn.

As soon as she reached her room she closed the door softly, so as not to disturb her governess, and heaved up the lid of the carved oak chest at the end of her bed. She had a moment's fear that the petticoat had been thrown out by her aunt — but no, there it was, woven from grey wool by Bridget, as soft and warm and comforting as Bridget herself. Thankfully Grace took the starched, prickly ruff from her neck and laid it on the bed; then she slipped off her over-mantle, carefully eased her arms out of the close-fitting sleeves of her underdress and pulled it over her head, and tugged off her starched linen petticoat. At last she stood in her shift. It felt lovely to put on the old petticoat again — it was almost as good as going home.

She put on her old grey cloak and pulled its hood over her brown curls. If her governess did happen to notice her, she would probably think that Grace was one of the serving-maids from the kitchen.

'Deirdre,' said Grace as they walked down the fields together, 'what did happen to my father and my mother? Why did they die?'

'Lord save us, child,' said Deirdre, making the sign of the cross rapidly, 'why do you ask me questions like that?'

'I don't know,' said Grace in a low voice. 'I thought I might have heard something .... Maybe I was having a bad dream.'

'That's it, lovey, just a bad dream. Don't you think

any more about it. Just say a prayer for them if you think of them. They're in heaven now, looking down on you.'

Grace said no more. She was learning very quickly that all her thoughts had to be kept to herself. Will Bridget be like this now? she wondered. Will she have changed in these few days?

'Isn't it a lovely day, Deirdre?' she said in her most grown-up way.

'It is indeed, thank God,' said Deirdre, obviously relieved at the change of subject.

That was the right thing to say, then, thought Grace. She looked around her. It actually was a lovely day. The icy winds of March were over; April was here, and there were clumps of pale lemon primroses in the mossy ditches and bright gold marsh marigolds beside the river. And best of all, she was going to see Bridget again. Bridget would listen to her and tell her what to do. Suddenly Grace felt quite sure of that. She knew she could trust Bridget.

In a little rocky field, just where the River Fergus tumbled down the rocks in a miniature waterfall, there was a group of blackthorn bushes. They had never been cut down, as they provided shelter for cattle in bad weather. When Grace had pushed through the gap, she could see that they made a perfect little hidden house, carpeted with moss and ivy and roofed with starry white. And in the middle, sitting on a moss-covered rock, was Bridget.

Grace flung herself on Bridget's lap and cuddled against her shoulder. Before she could stop herself, she popped her thumb in her mouth, just as if she were a baby again. She quickly pulled it out with a little plop and looked at Deirdre to see whether she had noticed, but Deirdre was busy talking to Bridget about the weather and about calves, so Grace popped her thumb back in again. It did feel comforting, and she was sure that Bridget would not scold her.

She wished Deirdre would go away. It would be hard to talk properly to Bridget while she was there. Grace took a last suck of her thumb and then sat up straighter.

'I can come back by myself, if you like, Deirdre,' she said. 'I know the way now, and no one will notice me. I'll keep my hood up and let it cover my face a bit.'

Deirdre laughed. 'Oh, you want to get rid of me and have Bridget all to yourself,' she said good-humouredly. 'Well, don't stay too long, and make sure your governess doesn't see you.'

There was a silence after she had gone. Grace found that after all, she did not really want to talk to Bridget; she just wanted to sit on her knee and suck her thumb, like a baby.

Bridget looked down at her little foster-child and stroked the brown curls. She didn't know what to do. She loved Grace as much as if she were a child of her own, as much as if she were that little daughter who had died just before Grace had come to her. Bridget wished she could just carry Grace back to the cottage by Lough Fergus, but she knew that was impossible. She was poor and unimportant. The Fitzgeralds would evict her from her cottage if they had any trouble, and that would do no good to anyone. For the child's sake, she had to do and say the right thing.

Bridget thought hard and carefully, and when she spoke her voice was calm and reassuring.

'Listen to me, Grace,' she said. 'Listen carefully. Come to the edge of the bushes with me; I want to show you something.'

Grace obediently stood up. Still keeping her thumb in her mouth and a tight hold on Bridget's hand, she peered out of the leafy house.

'You see the river there, the Fergus,' continued Bridget. 'Well, that river rises out of the ground in our own Lough Fergus, so if you walk along the bank there for half an hour or so, you'll come to the cottage. Do you see? You can't get lost if you keep by the Fergus.'

Grace nodded. Bridget smiled at her.

'So, you see,' she continued, 'every time your aunt goes out paying visits or going to Galway — and if I know that lady, that's where she'll spend most of her time — then you can just walk along by the river and visit me. I'll get out my best dishes for you, and you'll have a meal with me and play with Enda and help him with the horse.'

Grace pulled her thumb out of her mouth and stood up straight. She was beginning to like the sound of this.

Bridget took her by the hand and led her back to the moss-covered stone. She seated herself on it and lifted Grace back onto her knee. Her voice was calm and encouraging, with a world of certainty behind it.

'You see, Grace,' she said, 'things don't always work out the way we want them to. Now, you'd like to stay with me and I'd like to keep you, but there is no way that can happen, so we'll just have to make the best of it. You were always a clever little thing; by the time you were three years old you were as clever as Enda, and he five years older than you. Now you'll have to be very clever indeed. You'll have to do your best to pretend. Pretend you like living in the castle, pretend to be very grown-up and well-behaved; and if you go on pretending, it will become true. Your aunt has got a governess for you, so you must study and work hard, and whenever you have free time you can come over and tell me all about what you've learned. Make sure you get plenty of fresh air. If anything is wrong with you, tell Deirdre, and I'll send over some of my special herb-medicines. You'll see Enda when he comes over to the castle, but just pretend you don't know him if your aunt or uncle are anywhere around. Now, do you understand what you have to do?'

Grace nodded. She felt rather proud that Bridget thought she was clever. I *will* be clever, she thought, and I'll find some way of getting away from that horrible woman.

'Now may God bless you,' said Bridget solemnly. 'And may His holy Mother look after you and keep you in her care. You go on now. I'll stay a while, until you're back at the castle.'

CHAPTER THREE

And that was how Grace lived her life for the next five years. She became a silent, secretive child, flitting up and down the stairs like a little shadow, only really able to be herself when she escaped over to the little cottage by Lough Fergus. Usually, she only did that if her aunt and uncle were going to be away for at least a day; but on the day of her twelfth birthday, she was given a rare holiday from her studies and told that she could amuse herself for the afternoon. So she took a chance and went over to see Bridget and Enda.

It was a beautiful day in June. The air was filled with the scent of new-mown hay, and pale pink dog-roses bloomed in the hedges. Grace had a lovely afternoon. Bridget had baked a cake, in the hope that she would be able to come, and after they had all eaten it, Grace went fishing in Lough Fergus with Enda.

He was now a big strong boy of seventeen, able to do all the farm work for his widowed mother, and it wasn't often that he took time off to do something like fishing; so they were both enjoying the afternoon, until Enda spoke.

'Grace,' he said, 'they were saying at the market in Kilfenora that your uncle is selling three hundred acres of land.'

'I didn't know he even owned three hundred acres of land,' said Grace. 'Deirdre is always telling me he has nothing of his own.'

'It's not his land that he's selling,' said Enda. 'It's your land.'

'What!' Grace sat up straight in alarm. 'He can't do that!'

'Who is there to stop him?' said Enda softly.

There was a silence. Grace was no seven-year-old child now, and she immediately recognised the truth of what Enda was saying. There was no one to stop her aunt and uncle. She had only a few friends in the world, and all of them were poor and powerless.

Grace gritted her teeth. 'I don't care,' she said hotly. 'He's not going to get away with this. Could I borrow your horse, Enda, and ride to Ennis to find a lawyer?'

Enda looked at her in horror. 'You can't do that, Grace,' he said. 'No one will believe you if you just ride in on that big old carthorse and tell a story like that. Have some sense.'

'I suppose you're right,' said Grace slowly. 'I wonder if I could trust my governess. She's quite nice to me; she's always telling me how pleased she is with my studies, and how I'll become as clever as Queen Elizabeth if I carry on the way I'm going.'

'Would she risk offending your aunt?' asked Enda quietly.

Grace scowled, but she knew he was right.

'What can I do, then?' she asked.

'Just carry on, I suppose,' said Enda uncertainly. 'I don't really think you can do anything else. I'm sorry I told you, now.'

'That's all right,' said Grace drearily. 'I'd prefer to know, really.' After a moment she said: 'Enda, how long is it before I'm the owner of my own property? How long will I have to have them for my guardians?'

'Well, you can get married when you're fourteen, I think, and then they wouldn't be your guardians any more. I'll marry you, if you like.'

'Are you serious?' Grace sat up with her eyes shining. This seemed too good to be true. 'That would only be another two years. I think I could stand that. Are you really serious?'

'Of course he's serious,' said Bridget, coming up behind them and placing a hand on her son's shoulder. 'Hasn't he been in love with you since the day you came into this house? That's what you'll do, the pair of you. You'll get married in two years' time, and you'll live with me or in the castle, just as you like.'

Grace smiled happily. She had a slight uneasy feeling at the back of her mind that Bridget was just humouring her, trying to keep her cheerful and happy, and certainly Enda looked most uncomfortable — but then, he might just be shy. However, during the past five years, Grace had learned to take each day as it came and not to worry about the future, so she put all uncertainties out of her mind.

'Will we have a wedding party?' she asked eagerly.

'The best in the world,' Bridget assured her. 'We'll invite all the neighbours and have a big feast, with dancing and singing and music playing all the time.'

'And what will I wear?' asked Grace, trying to prolong the happy moment.

'Well, what would you wear, except the prettiest dress you have in your chest?' replied Bridget. 'Let's see, now, would it be the pink or the blue?'

'The pink,' said Grace decidedly.

'You've got a bite on your line,' said Enda hastily. 'Do you want me to reel it in for you?'

'No, I don't,' said Grace indignantly, all thoughts of her wedding going out of her head. 'I'll do it myself. I'm just as good as you at fishing. Just you watch.'

It was a beautiful trout, big enough to make a good supper for Enda and Bridget. As Grace skipped happily back along the river meadows, she had pushed the worrying news about her uncle to the back of her mind. She had hidden her shoes and stockings in the little house of blackthorn bushes on her way out; before going back to the castle, she carefully washed the dust from her feet in the river and put them back on.

As she came up the meadow in front of the castle, she could hear the sound of loud voices from the courtyard. There was her uncle's harsh voice and the flat tones of her aunt, but there was also another voice — a strange voice, big and booming.

Visitors, thought Grace, with some apprehension. She glanced down at her dress, to make sure that she was as clean and tidy as she had been when she set out, and then went bravely in through the big iron gates.

She wondered who the man with the big voice might be. I've never seen him before, she thought — and then she forgot all about him, because in front of the stables Joe was walking up and down leading the most beautiful pony Grace had ever seen. It was a palomino pony; its gleaming hide was a golden brown and its silky mane was the palest gold.

'Oh, Joe,' breathed Grace, her voice not much more than a whisper. She went across to the pony and rubbed its velvety nose. The pony whinnied with delight and bent its head down, snuffling at her hair.

'Grace!' Her aunt's voice recalled her, and she

went up the steps quickly.

'Grace, this is your father's cousin, Brendan Davoren.'

Grace dropped a curtsey, trying to remember all that her governess had taught her. She did not often meet her aunt's visitors, so she was not sure what to say. She glanced shyly up at her father's cousin. He was a very big man with brown eyes and brown curly hair and beard, dressed in very fashionable clothes. He looks kind, thought Grace, as he took her hand and helped her to rise.

'Well, Grace!' he boomed. 'I haven't seen you since you were seven years old.' He looked at her in a puzzled, slightly concerned way. 'You certainly have changed since then.' He turned to her aunt: 'Has she been ill? '

'No,' said Mary Fitzgerald, with a touch of bitterness in her voice. 'Grace is never ill.'

'So you're well and happy, then?' said Brendan Davoren to Grace.

Grace did not know what to say, so she just looked at him silently.

Then Brendan Davoren's face lit up with a big smile.

'I almost forgot,' he said. 'I have a present for you.'

Grace curtsied again. She did not really care too much what the present was — probably some sweet-meats. Whatever it was, her aunt would probably take it away and keep it for herself.

'Don't look like that,' he said teasingly. 'It's not every day that a girl's given a pony.'

'A pony!' For a moment Grace stared at him incredu-lously; and then she suddenly understood. She looked

back at the beautiful palomino pony, and saw Joe grinning from ear to ear. She could hardly believe it.

'For me?' she gasped.

He nodded — and to her own immense surprise, for the first time in years, Grace burst into tears.

Brendan knelt on the ground beside her and put his arm around her. 'What's wrong?' he said quietly.

Grace found it hard to control herself. The tears kept welling up, and she badly wanted to beg this kind man to take her away from this terrible place; but a dark shadow fell across her, blocking the sunlight, and she realised that her aunt had moved near. A thousand thoughts darted through her mind. He might believe her — but if he did not, she would be in a worse position than ever. Her aunt would beat her, perhaps lock her up ....

Grace remembered Bridget's words. She had to be brave and clever. She dried her tears, looked up into the concerned brown eyes so near to her own, and did her best to smile her prettiest smile.

'Nothing's wrong,' she said. 'I was just so surprised and delighted. Is the pony really mine, really just for me?'

'Really yours,' he said with a relieved smile.

'And will I be allowed to keep him, Aunt?' pursued Grace. She could see that her aunt was uneasy in this big man's presence. I'd better get everything fixed up before he goes, she thought.

'Of course you will be allowed to keep him,' snapped her aunt. 'But you can't ride, and I don't want you hurting yourself.'

'That's no problem,' said Brendan confidently. 'Joe will teach her to ride. It's time she learned. If she's anything like her father and mother, she'll be a good rider. When you can ride well, Grace, Joe will accompany you over to my house in Liscannor, by the sea, and you can meet my daughter Judith. She would like to meet you, and she'll be glad to see her pony again.'

He turned to Mary Fitzgerald and said in a low voice, 'It will be good for the child to meet other children. She must be lonely here.'

Mary nodded graciously, but said nothing.

She'll never allow me to go, thought Grace. Aloud, she said: 'Doesn't my cousin Judith want this pony, then?'

'She's grown too big for him,' explained Brendan. 'You'll be just right for him for another year or two, and then you'll have to pass him on to some other little girl. A pony must be ridden, or he gets fat and lazy and unhappy. When I get back I'll tell Judith that you love the pony, so she won't worry about him. She'll know he's in good hands.'

'Well, come inside and have some refreshment before you go,' said Mary. 'Grace, your governess is waiting for you in the library. And when you have finished your lessons, you had better have your supper and go directly to bed. You seem tired.'

Grace did not dare go back to pet the pony in front of her aunt, but when she reached the door she turned and looked back at him, standing there in the slanting rays of the evening sunshine. Joe gave a hasty glance at Mary Fitzgerald and then a huge wink at Grace. Grace smiled back. Joe was her friend and so was Deirdre, but now she had a new friend: the most beautiful pony in the world.

CHAPTER FOUR

$\mathfrak{G}$race slept very little that night, and by four o'clock in the morning she knew she would sleep no more. Pulling her lace nightcap from her tangled head, she opened the curtains of her four-poster bed and climbed down onto the cold stone floor. Shivering slightly, she crossed the room and pushed open the window. Her room faced north; but by leaning out as far as she dared, she could just see that the June dawn had already begun. As Grace watched, the sky turned from grey to pink, and then to a shade of pale gold as exquisite as her new pony's coat. That's it, Grace thought, that's his name: Golden Dawn.

Dressing herself quickly and carrying her leather shoes in her hand, Grace cautiously raised the latch of her bedroom door and crept down the spiral staircase.

As she pushed open the door of the stables, several sleepy horses raised their heads and there was a general chorus of whinnying; Grace was a great favourite with the horses. There in their boxes were the great farm horses which ploughed the fields and drew turf from the bog; there were the four handsome greys who drew the carriage; there was her father's old stallion, Sultan; but best of all, in the last box was her very own beautiful pony, Golden Dawn.

With no feeling of fear, Grace slipped into the box and began stroking the pony gently. He had been beautifully groomed; his golden hide was smooth and glossy and his blond mane was silky. Grace ran her hand down each leg in turn, just as she had seen Joe do, and checked each foot. He had been newly shod, she decided, and his feet were as well-cared-for as the rest of him. She stood with her arm around her pony, dreaming of the wonderful times she would have riding him across the fields, over the hills — perhaps even down to the sea .... All her worries about her uncle and aunt were pushed to the back of her mind; she thought only of her pony.

An hour later, the door of the stables was pushed open and Joe came in.

'What's got you up so early in the morning?' he asked, amused.

'Oh, Joe, do you think I could ride him?'

'That's a lovely little pony you've got there. Don't worry, we'll soon have you riding him. There's an old side-saddle your aunt used when she was about your size; I'll get it down from the loft and we'll give it a good clean.'

'I wish I didn't have to have a saddle,' muttered Grace. 'I never do when I'm with Enda.'

'I don't know how you manage in that dress, with the big wide skirt of it.'

Grace looked around carefully, then whispered: 'I don't wear a dress, Joe, I wear a pair of Enda's old breeches. You can't imagine how comfortable they are.'

'Well, I never heard of such a thing in all my life,' said Joe with a shocked air, though Grace could see that he was really trying to hide a smile. 'I don't know what Bridget is about, to let you do a thing like that.'

'Oh, I do what I like when I'm with Bridget,' said Grace. 'She nearly always lets me have my own way. It's nice to be spoiled by her for a while. I'm certainly not spoiled here,' she added, with a note of bitterness creeping into her voice.

'Well, don't think about that now,' said Joe. 'Let's go up to the loft and get this saddle down. I'll just dust it now, but later on, when you're having your lessons, I'll get young Martin to give it a good going-over with some saddle soap. We'll have it as good as new.'

Together they went up to the loft. They found the side-saddle under a pile of old cloths; it was still fairly supple, and Joe rubbed it vigorously with a wash-leather until it shone.

Grace looked at it thoughtfully. It was difficult to imagine Mary Fitzgerald as a young girl, the same age as herself, riding around the countryside at Drumshee.

'Joe, what was my aunt like when she was young?' she asked.

Joe gave a cautious glance around. 'Not too different from the way she is now,' he said briefly. 'A bit sour, like.'

Grace giggled. 'She's very sour, like, now,' she said.

'Just you be careful,' warned Joe. 'Don't let this pony go to your head. Keep nice and quiet and you won't get into trouble.'

Grace hung her head. Wouldn't it be lovely to be able to say exactly what she thought, rather than always having to keep a watch on her tongue!

'Come and help me tack him up,' said Joe

consolingly. 'I'll show you how, and then you'll be able to do it yourself whenever you want to go for a ride. Lead him out into the yard for me.'

Grace took the halter and led the pony out, stroking him reassuringly and rubbing his velvety nose.

'He's lovely, isn't he, Joe?'

'He's a beauty,' said Joe heartily. 'Now, you just keep talking to him while I put this on. He's used to a side-saddle, of course. Your cousin Judith would have had one on him for the last few years. There's a beauty — just stand still while I tighten the girths ....'

'Help me up on him, Joe,' said Grace, who could hardly stand still with excitement. 'I want to ride him.'

'Up you go,' said Joe, giving her a knee up. 'There! How does that feel? '

'Terrible,' gasped Grace. 'I don't think I'll ever get used to this saddle. I keep trying to grip with my knees, but there's nothing to grip.'

'Just hook your right leg over the pommel. It's easy once you get the feel of it. It's the safest way to ride. That's right — now put your left foot in the stirrup. Sit up and sit straight. Face forward.'

Grace felt very awkward, sitting there with one leg hooked around the pommel — which was a cushioned spike sticking up at the side of the saddle — and her other leg hanging uselessly at the pony's side. But after a little while she began to see the truth of what Joe had said: the pommel did hold her very securely. After about an hour, Grace began to feel quite confident with the side-saddle, and she urged the pony into a trot. Joe looked out from the stable, where he was busy grooming Sultan, and spoke to her in a low voice.

'Keep him walking. Remember, you're supposed to have learned to ride just this morning. *She* may be up by now, and if she looks out the window and sees you trotting she may suspect you've been going over to Bridget and Enda.'

Grace immediately slowed down to a walk. It was as well that she did: five minutes later the door to the castle opened and her aunt came out, followed by Joan the governess.

'Oh, Grace, how well you're riding!' exclaimed Joan. 'No one would ever imagine that this is your first time on a horse.'

'Rubbish,' snapped Mary Fitzgerald. 'She's got a very poor seat. Sit up straighter, child. '

Grace said nothing. She obediently tried to look as if she were sitting straighter. She knew that she was already as straight as she could be — it was one of the first things which Enda had taught her — but she also knew that it was worse than useless to argue with her aunt. It was also important not to look as if she was enjoying herself too much, or her aunt would find some reason to stop the riding lessons.

'That's enough, Grace,' said Mary abruptly. 'We must not let this riding interrupt your studies. What do you think?' she added, turning to the governess. 'Can she spare the time?'

'Oh, yes,' beamed Joan. 'Grace is a wonderful student. She's so clever, and she works so hard. In fact, I think she works too hard — it worries me sometimes. A horse is just what she needs. The Queen herself always recommends horseback riding. It gives a graceful carriage and aids the digestion, she says.'

Grace silently gave thanks for the Queen of England. Normally, she was extremely bored by her governess's hourly references to Her Majesty, but now they saved the day for her. With a curt nod, Mary turned and went indoors.

'I think you'd better come in to your studies,' said Joan nervously. 'Your aunt would like you to, I think. But you can ride again in the afternoon.'

Grace dismounted and followed her governess up the winding stone staircase to the library. Usually she did not mind studying; she did not find it hard, and while her mind was busy with her books she did not trouble about other things. Today, however, the hours dragged. She kept thinking about her beautiful Golden Dawn. She longed to be with him, to feel his silky mane under her fingers, to smell the clean smell of a well-groomed horse; and above all she longed to ride him properly — not just to walk up and down the yard, but to gallop across the fields.

When lessons were over, Grace flew down to the kitchen to eat her meal. Deirdre, who had heard all about the pony, had placed two apples beside Grace's plate. 'One for you and one for the horse,' she said, beaming all over her broad face.

'So you met your father's cousin, Brendan Davoren, then,' she added.

'Yes,' said Grace, with her mouth full of bread. She was always hungry after lessons. 'Do you know him, Deirdre?'

'I remember him coming here a few times. That would be quite a few years ago. A big man, isn't he? He'd be one that you could trust.'

Grace was silent for a moment. I wonder, she thought. She said carelessly: 'He asked me to ride over to visit his daughter Judith some time.'

'Will *she* let you go?' asked Deirdre, her eyes doubtful.

'I don't know,' said Grace. 'Probably not. Is it a long way to Liscannor? He said it was by the sea.'

'I don't know, love. I've never been there.'

I'll ask Enda, thought Grace. He'll know. Aloud, she said, 'Is that the carriage? Are my aunt and uncle going out? '

'Yes, they're going to Galway, the pair of them, thank God. They're going visiting. You can enjoy your ride in peace.'

Grace flew out of the kitchen and dashed into the stables, singing to herself. It made such a difference when her aunt and uncle were out!

'Joe,' she called, 'Joe, may I take my pony down to the Big Meadow? They've finished cutting the hay there. I won't do any harm.'

Joe looked troubled. 'I'll be the one who'll get into trouble if anything happens to you,' he said. 'I don't like you going down there on your own. You might have a fall.'

'Oh, please let me, Joe,' pleaded Grace. 'I can ride very well, really! I'm always riding, every time I go over to Bridget's.'

Joe continued to look troubled. 'I'd go with you myself, but I have a lot to do here and young Martin has had to go home. His father had a bad fall.' He looked at her downcast face and then said, 'Oh, well, I suppose you can't come to much harm on the grass. Take care, now — no wild riding.'

'Oh, thank you!' said Grace. Without giving him a chance to change his mind, she turned the pony's head and trotted him down the avenue, under the shade of the ancient oaks, and out into the sunshine of the Big Meadow.

The pony seemed to enjoy the feeling of the grass under his feet, after the rough cobbles of the courtyard, and he began to go a little faster. Grace sat up straight, with her head held high and the summer sun on her back, and felt that life was wonderful.

They had almost reached the little stream on the other side of the meadow when suddenly a hare started up, almost under the pony's feet. Golden Dawn reared, Grace instinctively clutched his mane, and the pony took off. Hedges, ditches, grass and hill all began to merge in her eyes as the pony bolted. At

first she was afraid she would fall off; then she almost began to hope that she would. They were galloping towards the stream.

I must make him stop, Grace thought frantically. Remembering what Enda had told her, she let go of the pony's mane and began to pull the reins steadily. Golden Dawn, however, took no notice. On and on he flew, and the stream came nearer and nearer.

I mustn't get killed, Grace told herself, I must not get killed or Joe will be blamed. After all, I only have to hold on and I'll be safe. I'm sure Judith has taught Golden Dawn how to jump.

She held on tight. As they approached the stream, the pony's stride lengthened and he seemed to surge beneath her. At the moment that Golden Dawn leaped over the stream, Grace heard a skylark, far above her head, break into song.

For the rest of my life, she thought, I will remember this moment: my golden pony flying through the air with me, and overhead the skylark singing.

Golden Dawn landed neatly and safely on the other side of the stream and began to gallop up the hill on the far side, towards the old stone rings which had been used, in ancient times, to enclose the cattle. He was not going so fast any more; the hill was quite steep and it slowed him down. Grace didn't care how far or how fast he went. She felt she could gallop with him to the end of the earth.

CHAPTER FIVE

Grace's aunt and uncle did not return that evening, and Deirdre said they were staying in Galway for a few days.

'You mark my words,' she said happily, 'we won't see them before the week is out. She's been restless for the last week, walking around finding fault with everyone. You'll be able to go riding tomorrow, lovey. I'll ask that governess if you can be having a bit of a holiday. You spend too much time at those books of yours.'

'Oh, wouldn't it be lovely!' said Grace. 'I'd love to go for a proper ride.'

'You can't go by yourself,' said Joe firmly. 'You're not properly used to that pony yet. It wouldn't be safe.'

'Oh, Joe,' Grace began — but then the door opened and Enda came in, carrying a few pounds of Bridget's butter, which she sold to the castle. A wonderful idea came to Grace.

'Oh, Enda,' she said, 'could you spare the time to come riding with me tomorrow? I've got the most beautiful pony you've ever seen. I've called him Golden Dawn. I got him from my father's cousin, Brendan Davoren — Golden Dawn used to be his daughter's pony, but she grew too big for him, so he brought him over yesterday evening for me. Please, Enda, do come with me! Joe says I can't go by myself.'

Enda nodded. 'I'll have to do the milking first,' he

said, 'but I'll be around after that. There isn't too much to do at the moment, now we've finished the haymaking. Do you want to show me the pony now?'

'Oh yes,' said Grace happily, leading him out to the stables. Enda's face lit up when he saw Golden Dawn. Grace had known that he would love him. Enda was an excellent rider, and horses were his great love.

'Are you able to ride him all right?' he asked, stroking the pony, who nuzzled up against him.

Grace looked around to make sure that Joe had not come back from the kitchen, and then said: 'I even jumped with him. It was a bit of a mistake, really. A hare frightened him and he bolted, and then we jumped the stream together.'

'Did you fall off?'

'No, of course not! But let me tell you, it's difficult riding with that side-saddle. I bet you wouldn't like it.'

'I'd look funny, wouldn't I?' said Enda with a grin. 'Anyway, I'll be over in the morning, so I'll see you then.'

Grace went to bed that night feeling blissfully happy. She was up with the lark, but she resolutely fought down the desire to go straight to the stables. As soon as she had had her drink of milk and slice of bread from the kitchen, she went straight to the library; by the time her governess arrived she had already done two hours' work, and her neatly-written Latin exercises and her French translation were lying on the ancient oak table.

'You're a good child,' said Joan. 'The cook has begged me to give you a little holiday today, so you can enjoy your new pony, and I'm happy to do that, especially since you've already done so much work.'

'I'll do my mathematics now and practise my music,' said Grace, 'and then I'll have finished.'

She glanced out of the library window. The sun was high in the sky; Enda should have finished the milking and all of his morning tasks by now. Grace bent her curly head over the rows of figures, her quick brain disentangling their complexities with an ease born of study and practice. By the time the door opened and Deirdre came in, Grace had finished her day's work .

'Come into the kitchen before you go,' whispered Deirdre. 'I have something for you.'

Enda was already in the kitchen when Grace came running in, and Deirdre, beaming all over her face, was handing him a wicker basket.

'That's something for your midday meal,' she said. 'Stay out all day and have a good time, the two of you.'

Out in the courtyard Martin, the stable-boy, was holding Golden Dawn; Joe had already saddled him and was checking the girths. Enda climbed up on the old white carthorse, with the wicker basket in front of him, and Grace mounted Golden Dawn. Riding sedately, the two of them set off down the avenue.

When they reached the gate to the Big Meadow, Enda stopped. By the gate were some bales of straw and a long pole. Enda climbed down from his horse and opened the gate.

'I was a bit worried when you told me that story about the hare frightening Golden Dawn,' he said seriously. 'I thought it might be a good idea for you to learn to jump properly, and Joe agrees with me. I'll do you a low one first, with just one bale on either side.'

'That's a baby jump,' said Grace scornfully.

'Well, do it perfectly and then I'll make it higher.'

Grace cantered forward and jumped nonchalantly, taking no particular care.

'Do it again,' ordered Enda. 'Lean forward when you jump.'

Grace glared at him, but took more care this time. Golden Dawn cleared the pole by several feet.

'That's better,' said Enda. 'Now we'll try two bales of straw.'

Again Golden Dawn jumped successfully.

'He's a great jumper, but you're not doing much to help,' said Enda.

'Well, how am I supposed to help him?' snapped Grace. 'I can only help him by getting off and letting him do it on his own.'

'No, silly, just lean forward. It helps your pony because you shift your weight from his back to his neck. Keep your own back in line with your pony's. I know it's not easy with that silly side-saddle, but try anyway.'

Grace did her best to follow his instructions, and this time Golden Dawn soared over the pole like a bird.

'Oh, that was a wonderful feeling!' she shouted. 'I'll do it again.'

She pulled the reins, galloped the pony back to the gate and came thundering up the dry, hard ground. She leaped over the pole again and again, until she was breathless.

'You try, now,' she gasped.

Enda laughed and shook his head. 'This fellow's jumping days are over. He's a great workhorse, and he might be able to jump if there was a need for it, but he wouldn't see the point of jumping over a pole when he could walk around it.'

'I wish you could have a proper horse, Enda,' said Grace. 'A stallion like my father's. You're a great rider.'

'Well, I don't see myself getting that sort of money,' said Enda calmly. 'I'm lucky to have this old boy. Let's put these bales and the pole under the hedge, here. Joe says we can keep them there, so you can practise whenever your aunt and uncle aren't around. I'll tell you what we'll do now; we'll ride along the lanes towards Ennis. It's a lovely road, and you've never been along it.'

It was a beautiful ride. The sun shone, the wild roses filled the hedges, and the tangled woodbine gave out a strong sweet perfume which filled the air.

By midday it was getting very hot, and Grace and Enda stopped in the shade of a thick hedge, beside an ivy-covered spring well. They tied the two horses to an old ash tree and allowed them to crop the sweet juicy grass which grew in the shade, and they opened the wicker basket.

'Look at this,' said Enda, delving into it. 'Chicken legs, four of them! And two little pies.'

'And fresh raspberries!' exclaimed Grace. 'They're my favourite fruit. What's in the package?'

'Deirdre's porter cake,' gloated Enda, who was mad about sweet things. 'And she's put buttermilk in a lidded jug.'

'I hope it's still all right, after all this heat.'

'Oh, yes, it will be,' said Enda confidently. 'She's packed wet moss all around it. I'll just put it into the well to get it really cold, though, while we're eating.'

'This is fun,' said Grace, sighing in contentment. 'If only every day could be like this day.'

'You wouldn't enjoy it so much if it were,' said Enda, but he spoke absentmindedly and his eyes were on a cloud of dust in the distance.

'That's a carriage coming,' he said. 'Who can it be?'

Grace sprang to her feet with a cry of alarm. 'Oh, no!' she said. 'It's the Fitzgeralds! They've come back early. Oh, quick, I must hide!'

'It's too late,' said Enda. 'That hedge is too thick to get through, and what would we do with the horses? They're bound to recognise Golden Dawn.'

Grace shut her eyes in agony — and opened them a minute later as there came a dreadful squealing, a crashing of hoofs, and a skidding of carriage wheels. Tom, the coachman, was doing his best to hold the magnificent greys while they plunged and reared; John Fitzgerald was shouting 'What the devil?' over and over again; and Mary was screaming 'Grace, who is this — ?'

They heard no more; at that moment the greys became too much for Tom to hold. They bolted, with the carriage swaying and bouncing behind them. Grace held her breath in horror, but a couple of minutes later the carriage came to the start of a long steep hill; bit by bit, the horses slowed down, and Grace could see that Tom had got back control over them. She gave a sigh of relief, and then a groan.

'Oh, Enda,' she said, 'what am I going to do? She was furious. She might take Golden Dawn away from me.'

'Oh, just keep out of her way for a few hours,' advised Enda. 'She'll calm down. Do you remember that time you persuaded me to take the pig for a walk, and he escaped and got into the cabbage garden? You remember how cross Mammy was then? We kept out of her way all day, and by the time we got home in the evening she'd almost forgotten all about it.'

Grace could not help laughing; she remembered Bridget, in her long black dress, with her shawl trailing off one shoulder and a stick in her hand, chasing that enormous muddy pig, a large cabbage sticking out of one corner of his mouth. Grace knew that her aunt was a very different person from Bridget, but she tried to tell herself that Enda might be right.

They spent the next few hours together, but Grace could no longer enjoy herself. She thought she might wait until dinnertime to slip into the stables with Golden Dawn, and then go up to her room after she had unsaddled him and rubbed him down. She never had meals with her aunt and uncle anyway, and with some luck she might be able to avoid them for a few days.

Luck was not on her side, however. When Grace came into the courtyard, walking quietly and leading Golden Dawn so that his hoofs would not make too much noise, she could see the tall angular figure of her aunt at the window of the Great Hall. In a flash, Mary Fitzgerald was out in the courtyard, with the governess beside her. She was in a towering rage.

Question after question and accusation after accusation were screamed at Grace. She stood with her head bowed and her heart thumping with fear, gently stroking Golden Dawn's silky hide and praying fervently that her aunt would not take her pony away.

I hate you, I hate you, I hate you, Grace thought over and over again. She wished she had the courage to say it aloud. But Grace had no courage now — Grace, who had been so brave and so fearless when she was a little child. She could only stand there, filled with a sick loathing, turning her eyes away from the spittle that gathered in the corner of that thin merciless mouth and trying to close her ears to the sound of that shrill voice. She hates me, Grace thought. And then, with a little shock of surprise, she saw in her mind, as clearly as if they had been written in large black letters on white paper, the words:

She hates me enough to kill me.

A large number of servants had gathered around them, and something in their shocked silence began to strike Mary Fitzgerald. She wiped her mouth and smoothed down her coarse grey hair.

She looked thoughtfully at Golden Dawn. Grace could see that it was on the tip of her tongue to say that the pony must be sold, but something stopped her. Perhaps she was afraid that Brendan Davoren would come back. Instead, she rounded on the unfortunate governess, who stood there, bobbing curtseys in a frightened manner.

'It's obvious to me,' she said in icy tones, 'that this child has not enough to do if she is running wild around the countryside with farm boys. I don't know why we pay you if this is the sort of care that you take of our niece. From now on, Grace must spend at least nine hours a day at her studies. Make sure that she spends at least an hour each day studying etiquette, to teach her good manners.'

Grace turned away, sick with despair. Her aunt had allowed her to keep Golden Dawn, but with nine hours a day spent in lessons, Grace would never have time for him. Struggling to keep her self-control, she led the pony into the stables and began to take off his saddle.

Joe followed her.

'Don't fret,' he said in a low voice. 'I get up at six,

and the stable boys get up at six, but your aunt and your governess are still in their beds until past eight.'

Grace stared at him. Then, as she realised what he meant, the colour began to come back to her cheeks and her eyes filled with hope.

'I'll do it,' she whispered to Golden Dawn as she rubbed him down. 'I'll do it without fail, no matter how tired I am. I promise you, I'll get up every single morning, winter and summer, and take you for a ride before I have breakfast.'

Over the next eighteen months, Grace never failed to keep that promise. It was just as well that she did have some fresh air and exercise, because she had to work so hard at her books and her music that she had no time to spare during the day.

She came to be considered one of the most highly-educated, accomplished young ladies in the west of Ireland. She could speak four languages, write beautifully, sing, dance, and play the virginal and the lute. Everyone knew that; but only Joe and Enda knew that she was also one of the best riders in the countryside.

Although she was strong and healthy, Grace did not grow any bigger in that time; she was quite small for her age. Her aunt and uncle made scornful remarks about how small she was, but Grace did not mind. She knew that once she reached her fourteenth birthday she would probably not grow much more, and this meant that Golden Dawn would be the right size for her for the rest of his life. And Golden Dawn was more important to her than anything else at Drumshee.

CHAPTER SIX

One day in early November, in the year 1587, Grace and Enda were out riding early in the morning. Usually everything was quiet and still at that hour, but now they could hear the sounds of wagons and of men's voices shouting. Grace turned to Enda in alarm.

'I think it must be someone moving into Inchovea Castle,' said Enda. 'Someone told me the O'Briens had let it to an Englishman called Thompson.'

Inchovea Castle was about a mile to the east of Drumshee. It stood on a little island, surrounded by the river, and looked as if it had been built at about the same time as Drumshee.

'They'll have a lot to do to it,' observed Grace. 'It's been empty for years.'

They sat on their horses beside the waterfall, watching with interest. Great wagons full of furniture were trundling up the muddy lane, and the whole castle was alive with the noise of hammering and the cries of the servants.

As they sat there, Grace realised that she was being watched. A middle-aged man — richly dressed in the height of fashion, with a starched ruff around his neck and an embroidered jerkin of purple velvet — stood at an open casement and regarded her with interest.

'Oh dear,' said Grace. 'He's bound to come calling on my aunt and uncle. I hope he won't say anything about seeing me.'

51

'Do you have meals with them now?' asked Enda, as they made their way back towards Drumshee.

'Sometimes,' said Grace briefly. 'Deirdre told me that there was a lot of gossip about me, so now my aunt occasionally trots me out when there's a visitor.'

As they rode quietly across the fields, Grace wondered whether there was any chance that the Englishman would not recognise her. Unlikely, she thought; and of course, her uncle and aunt were bound to invite him to dinner. However, it was quite possible that she would not be invited to join them. She tried to put the unfortunate meeting out of her head and to concentrate on her lessons.

However, when she came out of the library that evening, with a throbbing headache from her nine hours of study, Grace found the castle in an uproar. Deirdre was roasting fowl over the great fires in the kitchen, the kitchen boy was scrubbing the vegetables, one of the maids was making sweetmeats from marzipan, and another was laying the table in the Great Hall with the finest linen tablecloth. Mary Fitzgerald herself was putting out the best silver and the finest glass, while John fetched bottles of French wine from the cellar. It appeared that William Thompson and his son Robert were, indeed, coming to dine at Drumshee.

Following a sharp order from her aunt, Grace dressed herself in her prettiest clothes: a pale green farthingale — a hooped petticoat — and a cream-coloured kirtle embroidered with yellow poppies. Her soft leather and satin slippers made no sound as she entered the Great Hall, and the three adults in front of the fireplace were unaware of her presence.

'I cannot see why you should object to my son, good sir,' William Thompson was saying to her uncle. 'As I said in my letter, there would be no question of an immediate marriage — simply a formal betrothal, an engagement to marry when the girl is fifteen. I have mentioned it to the Queen and she strongly approves.'

Grace stopped abruptly. They were talking about her.

A queer little thrill of excitement went through her. If she were married, she could escape from her aunt and uncle ....

However, one glance at the sulky young man standing at the window dampened that excitement. In spite of the fact that he, like his father, had just come from Queen Elizabeth's court and was dressed in the height of fashion, Grace could see that he was fat and pasty-faced. In her mind she contrasted him with Enda, who was slim and brown; and she knew that she did not want to marry Robert Thompson.

She coughed gently and moved over towards the group at the fireplace, and they all stopped talking.

William Thompson looked at her with amusement. 'So this is the little lady who rides around the countryside at seven o'clock in the morning,' he remarked.

Grace sank down in a deep curtsey, her face a mask of demure politeness, but her heart was beating wildly with terror. What would her aunt say afterwards? Now she had a very good excuse to get rid of Golden Dawn .... At least William Thompson had said nothing about Enda. He probably thought Enda was just one of her servants.

The meal seemed endless to Grace. Her aunt, for once, spoke very little; but every time Grace looked up from her plate, she found the woman's eyes fixed on her. From their expression, Mary Fitzgerald's mind was working busily.

Nothing was said after the visitors had gone; but Grace went to bed still feeling uneasy.

Grace was used to problems, and her way of dealing with them was to put them out of her head as soon as possible. So, with a great effort, she managed to fall asleep.

It was midnight, a black night with no stars, and the moon's face was hidden by ragged clouds when Grace woke up, suffocating. For a moment she thought she must be dreaming; then she realised that this was no nightmare. The curtains of her bed had been drawn back and a candle on the chest sent grotesque black shadows leaping on the white-washed ceiling. A rough woollen scarf had been wound around her mouth, and her arms and legs were tightly bound.

'For God's sake, let me kill her now and be done with it,' growled her uncle's voice. 'If we're forced to agree to this marriage contract, it will be discovered how much of her land has been sold!'

'Fool,' came Mary Fitzgerald's low steady voice. 'If we kill her now we will fall under suspicion. William Thompson will be suspicious, Brendan Davoren will be suspicious. I have released her pony from the stables. When he is found wandering loose, then, and only then, we will kill her. We will place her body at the bottom of the quarry and send out word that she is missing. We will have a great hunt for her, and

when the body is found everyone will believe that she went out riding early in the morning and fell and broke her neck. But until the pony is found, we will leave her in the cellar.'

When Grace heard these merciless words she knew that there was no escape for her. She could neither struggle nor beg; and even if she had not been gagged, no appeal could have changed her aunt's iron resolution. There was nothing she could do.

An icy chill came over her whole body as she felt herself being lifted from her bed. Great shudders shook every limb and she was suddenly soaked in sweat. There was a sound like the roaring of the waterfall in her ears, and Grace knew no more.

CHAPTER SEVEN

When Grace recovered from her faint she found that she was lying, wrapped in blankets, on the cold damp flagstones of the cellar. It was pitch dark, but Grace was so relieved to find herself alive that she began to feel a little better. She knew that she was in deadly danger, but now that her aunt and uncle were not with her, Grace was no longer paralysed with fear. She began to think about how she might escape.

It was still night, she guessed, or else there would be a chink of light coming from the tiny window in the top of the wall; and she could hear the sound of torrential rain beating against the castle walls.

Oh, poor Golden Dawn, Grace thought. The rain and wind will frighten him. Perhaps he'll make his way over to Lough Fergus and Enda will find him and come to rescue me.

In her heart Grace knew that there was little chance of Enda coming to rescue her, but the thought brought back her courage. She began to plan. If she could somehow cut the rope which bound her hands behind her back, she would be able to untie her ankles and take off the scarf around her mouth. Then perhaps she could climb up on some barrels of wine and reach the little window. She knew that the window was too small for her to climb through, but perhaps when Joe came to work in the morning she would be able to call to him.

Grace concentrated hard. From the sound of the

rain, she knew she was on the south side of the cellar, the side where the window was. Although she could see nothing, she could clearly picture the cellar. The south, west, and east walls were all built of smooth, well-squared stones which had been carefully placed on top of one another; but on the north side, half of the wall was filled in with rough uncut stones with jagged edges. Deirdre had once told Grace that she had heard that long, long ago there had been a secret way out of the castle through that wall ....

Secret way or not, Grace knew that she would not have the strength to pull out any of the stones. But

she might just be able to use one of the rough edges to cut the rope. Slowly and painfully, she managed to sit up with her back against the wall. Using her shoulders, she shrugged off the blankets — their warmth was comforting, but she needed freedom of movement. The daily hours of riding had made Grace's muscles strong; she was able to wriggle forward onto her knees, and then to stand up.

Inch by inch, keeping her bound hands against the wall, she edged her way along the east wall of the cellar. It seemed like hours before her right shoulder struck something hard and she knew that she had

reached the corner between the east wall and the north.

Moving jerkily, in a series of awkward hops, she turned the corner. Every step was an effort, and despite the fact that she was only wearing her night-gown, she could feel the sweat running down her forehead. Her breath came in great gasps.

However, a great surge of hope began to rise within her. I've managed so far, she thought, and surely I have only about six more feet to go before I reach the rough stones. She did not let her mind dwell on whether she would actually be able to cut the rope which bound her wrists; instead, she concentrated all her thoughts on the picture of Golden Dawn galloping across the hills, his pale golden tail streaming out behind him, galloping at great speed to bring her help from Bridget and Enda.

With that image in her mind, Grace struggled on until her hand struck what she was waiting for. It was the rough edge of a stone — so rough, in fact, that Grace could feel blood trickling down from the side of her hand where she had knocked against it. Edging a little nearer, she stood with her back to the stone and began the slow, painful process of rubbing her bound hands up and down against its edge.

Because she could not see what she was doing, she knocked her hands again and again. Soon she could feel the blood pouring down, and it became harder and harder to persevere. What made things even worse was that Grace had no idea whether or not she was managing to cut the rope. Every few minutes she stopped and tried to force her hands apart, but they remained as firmly bound as ever.

The pain from her cut and bruised hands was

nothing compared to the pain from the cramped muscles in her arms. The hope which had risen so strongly in her was beginning to fade.

And then disaster struck.

The stone which Grace had been rubbing her hands against — the narrow, sharp, protruding stone which was so ideal for her purpose — fell out of the wall, leaving only some piece of wire or metal in her hands.

Clutching it, Grace cried out in despair: 'Help me, someone, help me! Help me, for God's sake!'

Afterwards, Grace could never be sure whether the rope simply parted — or whether, as she firmly believed to the end of her days, that cry of agony echoed down through the centuries, through the corridors of time. There in front of her, holding a candle, stood a beautiful girl of Grace's own age. She was taller than Grace, with long black hair which hung down her back, and she wore a purple tunic. By her side stood an enormous dog, grey as a wolf. In her hand she held a strange iron knife. She smiled at Grace, and walked behind her.

'I see you have found my necklace,' she said.

The rope fell away from Grace's wrists. Still holding the piece of metal in her hand, she turned to face the girl who had released her.

The stone which had fallen out had left a gap in the wall, and a ray of moonlight shone through. Grace was alone; there was no trace of the strange girl.

At that moment, there was a sound of thudding blows on the outside of the wall, then a rumbling noise, and then a great crash. The piled stones collapsed, and a large, noble head with a blond mane appeared in the gap. It was Golden Dawn.

CHAPTER EIGHT

Golden Dawn was wearing his saddle and bridle; obviously Mary Fitzgerald had saddled him before turning him loose, so that it would look as if Grace had fallen off him while she was out riding. As soon as Grace had untied her ankles and clambered over the fallen stones, she held the pony's bridle and leaned against him, standing quietly in the shadow of the castle wall.

Surely the noise of the stones falling will have woken someone, she thought. She waited, her heart hammering against her ribs. No light shone from the castle, not a casement was opened, no voice was heard; but still she waited.

The rain had ceased; the full moon shone in a cloudless sky, and the ground behind the castle was as bright as day. Grace knew that if she moved she would be seen by anyone who had woken up, so she stayed as still as a statue.

She opened her hand and stared with curiosity at the strand of metal which lay there, glinting in the moonlight.

'I see you have found my necklace,' the girl in the strange clothes had said.

The object lying in Grace's hand was indeed a necklace, though of a strange design. The dust and dirt which covered it could not hide the fact that it was made from gold. Two delicate ribbons of pure gold had been twisted together; on one end there was a small loop, on the other a beautifully-ornamented hook which had been broken.

It must have been lost when that broke, Grace thought.

Several minutes had passed, and still there was no sound from the silent castle. Holding the necklace in her left hand and Golden Dawn's bridle in her right, Grace crept cautiously out through the ditch which surrounded the wall — the ditch which, more than a thousand years before, had surrounded an old fort where a girl called Nuala had lived.

Grace paused again before climbing out of the ditch. It was about fifteen feet lower than the castle courtyard, so no one could see her there; but once she was out in the moonlit field, any wakeful person would spot her easily.

However, Grace knew that she was getting steadily colder and colder. Luckily her nightgown was made of thick wool, but even so, the cold November night was beginning to chill the marrow of her bones. She knew she would have to take a chance. She dared not ride Golden Dawn, as the noise of his hoofs might awaken someone, so she led him quietly down the hillside to the sunken lane which ran between the fields. Once she reached the Rough Field, she climbed on to his back and urged him forward.

The past week had been a time of endless rain. Shower after shower had swept in from the west, the rain falling in slanted grey lines and the bare trees bending beneath its force. The heavy clay in the rushy fields was filled with water; the feet of the cattle had made muddy tracks and puddles, and Golden Dawn stumbled and almost fell.

Grace immediately slowed him down. Despite her frozen state and her terror, the pony always came first with Grace, and she was determined that no harm would come to him on this night ride. She stroked his golden neck gently and wondered at his loyalty. Ninety-nine horses out of a hundred, if they had been turned out of their stables in the middle of the night, would have galloped wildly across the countryside. But Golden Dawn had not; he had waited around the castle, and some instinct had led him to the place where the cellar wall backed on to the ditch. And when Grace had cried out, he had kicked at the crumbling stones. She owed her life to him.

Golden Dawn trotted on as quickly as he could, despite the heavy mud clinging to his hoofs. Up to the top of the hill near Kylemore he went, and then down the other side, across the fast-flowing River Fergus. Once they were out on the road, Grace was able to let him gallop until they reached the little stone cottage near Lough Fergus, the cottage where she had spent the first seven years of her life.

More dead than alive, Grace tumbled off the pony and led him up the path to the cottage door. It was a half-door, and during the day the top half was always left open, but tonight both halves were tightly shut against the wind and the rain. Grace banged on the door with her free hand, as loudly as she could, and stood there smelling the sharp scent of the turf smoke which was pouring out of the chimney. Bridget kept a turf fire burning day and night, and Grace had never known what it was to be cold until she went to the great gloomy castle of Drumshee.

There was a sound of voices from within, and then Bridget, wrapped in her black shawl, opened the door. Behind her, just visible in the light of the fire, Enda was hastily pulling on his breeches over his nightgown. With an exclamation of horror, Bridget undid the bottom half of the door and took Grace into her arms.

'Oh, Bridget, they tried to murder me — my aunt and uncle tried to murder me!'

'What are you saying, child? They couldn't — not your own flesh and blood!'

'They did, they tied me up and gagged me and put me in the cellar. Bridget, you must hide me, you must, they'll be coming after me!'

Over Grace's head, Bridget's eyes met Enda's, and there was a pause. Grace looked at them anxiously. Surely they were not going to abandon her — her only friends in the world!

Bridget's face wore the look that she had when she was thinking hard.

'Rub down that pony, Enda,' she said. 'Give him a drink, but don't give him anything to eat. Leave him in the cabin and then come in.'

'Come on, pet,' she added, turning to Grace. 'You're wet through and you're destroyed with the cold. Come in by the fire.'

An hour later, Grace was still in her foster-mother's arms, sitting cosily in front of the glowing fire. She had told her story of horror and treachery; now, with a glass of Bridget's elderberry wine warming her stomach, she felt as if everything which had happened to her that night had been just a bad dream. Her head fell back, her hazel eyes closed, and she slept as securely as she had when she was four years old.

It seemed as if she had only been asleep for two minutes when she felt herself being gently shaken awake. This is the second time I've been woken up tonight, she thought sleepily — but this time it was not to a nightmare of shadows and enemies, but to warmth and love and security.

'Child,' Bridget was saying, her brown eyes fixed intently on Grace, 'child, you can't stay here. It's the first place the Fitzgeralds will come looking for you. Enda's gone to saddle the pony and the horse; he'll ride with you to Brendan Davoren's house in Liscannor. Brendan Davoren is a good man, and he'll be able to keep you safe. Come now, put on this warm jerkin, and I have a pair of Enda's old breeches warming by the fire for you.'

Grace struggled out of Bridget's arms and stood up.

'Oh, Bridget,' she said, 'I wish I could be a baby again. I don't want to have to do things. I don't want to be hated. I don't want to be in danger.'

Bridget's soft brown eyes filled with tears. Her work-roughened hand gently stroked Grace's hair.

'It will be all right,' she said softly. 'Brendan Davoren will look after you. Just be brave for a while longer.'

Grace dressed herself as quickly as she could, slipping the necklace into the pocket of the jerkin. She had not said anything about the girl in purple; she could not decide whether to keep it a secret for ever.

She kissed Bridget and mounted Golden Dawn. Enda climbed up onto the broad back of the old carthorse, and side by side they galloped down the moonlit road.

They rode for some time in silence. Enda was looking very worried, and Grace guessed that he was afraid he would not be able to protect her if the Fitzgeralds tried to recapture her. After all, he was only eighteen years old. Grace herself, however, was not really worried. She still felt slightly drowsy, and she was happy to gallop along beside Enda and trust to her friend to look after her, after the terrors of the night.

Golden Dawn was happy as well, she felt. He must have been very frightened when he had been turned out of his stable and driven away in the middle of the night, but now he was back with Grace again, and he was allowed to go as fast as he could. He held his head high and matched the big carthorse stride for stride.

They rode side by side, making good time. Enda was still very tense; he kept looking over his shoulder. The moon was full, and the little road was as bright as day. They rode past Lake Lickeen, its water silvered and mysterious, and passed Smithstown Castle just as the clock in the stableyard chimed four o'clock.

Enda began to relax a little. We'll reach Liscannor in less than an hour, he thought, and there's no sign of anyone coming after us. The world seemed empty of everything except themselves, and there was no sound but the clip-clop of their horses' hoofs on the hard road.

Enda glanced at Grace and smiled. 'You're very quiet,' he said.

Grace did not reply for a minute. Then she said, slowly and thoughtfully, 'Enda, just before the cellar wall collapsed, something very odd happened. I saw a girl about my age, but dressed in a strange purple tunic. She was carrying a little iron knife, and I think she cut the rope from my wrists with it. She had a dog with her — at least, I think it was a dog; he was huge, like a wolf, but he stood beside her like a well-trained dog.'

Enda stared at her. 'You must have imagined it,' he said.

'I've been trying to tell myself that,' said Grace quietly, 'but I know it wasn't my imagination or a dream.'

'How can you be so sure?'

'Well, before the girl cut the rope, she said, "I see you have found my necklace." And when I got out of the cellar, I found this in my hand.'

Grace reined in her pony and brought the necklace out of her jerkin. 'Look at it, Enda. It could be more than a thousand years old. I'm sure it's made of gold.'

Enda's face was as white as the moon. 'It must have been a ghost from the past,' he said fearfully.

Grace thought for a while. 'I wasn't afraid of her,' she said. 'I felt as if she was my friend.'

They both began cantering along the road again, the hoofs making a pattern of sound which formed a background music to Grace's thoughts: Who was that girl? Will I ever see her again? Should I wear the necklace or hide it? Should I tell anyone else, or should I keep it a secret between me and Enda?

As if he could read her thoughts, Enda spoke.

'I think you shouldn't tell Brendan Davoren about this girl,' he said thoughtfully. 'If he doesn't believe in her, he might not believe you're telling the truth about the Fitzgeralds trying to murder you. And you know how important it is for Brendan Davoren to believe you. He's the only one who's powerful enough to protect you from the Fitzgeralds.'

Grace nodded. 'I think you're right,' she said. 'I was —' And then she stopped, her words checked in a gasp of horror.

While they were talking, their horses had been climbing the steep hill near Kilshanny. Now they had reached the top and could look down at the wide bay of Liscannor. The storm of the early part of the night had gone completely, but huge white-capped waves were still rolling in, and a heavy wooden ship, anchored by the black rocks, swung and tossed in the rough seas.

It was not that sight, however, which brought the terror back into Grace's eyes.

In the still, frosty air there was a metallic drumming sound which echoed the footfalls of their own horses. There were people riding up the road — and by the sound of them, these were no farmers coming back from a night's revelry in a neighbour's house, no party of men sent to fetch a priest to a deathbed. This was the sound of trained men, of soldiers riding in disciplined silence.

Quick as a flash, Enda slid off his horse. Holding the bridle, he squeezed through a gap in the hedge. Without hesitating, Grace followed.

They stood there, still as statues, while around the corner came a troop of soldiers. The men were dressed in full armour, and the moonlight gleamed on the silver plates which covered limbs and bodies. It was obvious that this was a ride with a purpose. As they went, the officer and his men continually scanned the fields on either side.

Grace and Enda pressed as close to the tall hedge as they could. Enda was praying that their horses would make no sound. His carthorse might possibly be taken for that of a local farmer, but if Grace's thoroughbred pony was seen, there would be no chance for them.

Grace was past praying; she was in a state of complete despair. The Fitzgeralds must have discovered her absence and sent a message to the military. She would be taken back to Drumshee, and the horror would begin all over again.

Enda squeezed her hand. He guessed what she was feeling, but he was powerless to help her.

Time seemed endless as the long column of soldiers passed their hiding place. When the last man finally rounded the corner, Enda and Grace still stood there, not daring to move until the sound of hoofbeats had died away.

'Do you think they were looking for me?' Grace's voice shook despite her efforts to keep it steady.

'I don't think so,' Enda said thoughtfully. 'It would be too soon for the Fitzgeralds to have sent a message over here. Tom told me the soldiers are keeping a watch all along the coast, because Queen Elizabeth is afraid that King Philip of Spain is going to send troops to Ireland. There are supposed to be thousands of huge Spanish ships sailing across the sea, and no one knows if they're going to land in Ireland or in England. I'm sure those soldiers were nothing to do with you. They would never send out so many armed men just to look for one girl. Just to be safe, though, we'll take that path across the fields to your cousin's place. It might be better to keep off the roads.'

They crossed the fields slowly and cautiously, keeping in the shadows of hedges and listening intently all the time. Though she had been slightly reassured by Enda's explanation, Grace was still very frightened. When they reached the tall black gates which led to Brendan Davoren's house, she broke into a wild gallop, only pulling up her pony in front of the stone steps which led to the great front door.

Tossing her bridle to Enda, she raced up the steps and hammered on the door with all her strength.

CHAPTER NINE

$\mathfrak{I}$t seemed like an age before anyone answered. Grace kept looking fearfully over her shoulder to see whether the soldiers had spotted them; her heart was thumping and her legs shaking by the time the heavy oak door was finally opened. An old man-servant stood there, with a candle in his hand; and behind him stood the strong figure of Brendan Davoren.

Grace did not hesitate: she brushed past the old man and threw herself into the arms of her father's cousin.

'Oh, help me, Cousin, help me!' she sobbed. 'Hide me from the Fitzgeralds. '

Brendan, holding her in his arms and patting her on the back, was looking horrified, but not as surprised as Grace had imagined he would be.

'May God forgive me for not going back to Drumshee to see how you were,' he said, as much to himself as to her.

Holding her by the shoulders, he looked keenly into her face; then, hugging her again, he looked over her head to where Enda stood, holding the two horses.

'Come in, lad,' he called to Enda.

'I dare not, sir. I've left my mother alone, and I must be back before the Fitzgeralds come searching for Grace. It will be dawn in two hours' time, and I must be back home before they discover she's escaped.'

Brendan frowned in puzzlement, but decided that explanations must wait.

'Give the lad a fresh horse from the stables, Robert,' he said to the stableman who had just appeared, 'and take care of my cousin's pony.'

'Enda's my foster-brother,' said Grace, as Brendan led her up the winding staircase.

'Tell me all presently,' said her cousin. 'But first we must find your cousin Judith. '

Judith Davoren was a tall girl of sixteen with a strong, kind face. She had the most beautiful hair Grace had ever seen; it was dull gold, rippling in tight waves down her back, to beyond her waist. Grace knew that Judith's mother, like her own, was dead; but unlike Grace, Judith had a father who was devoted to her.

Judith's bedchamber was as warm as a summer's night, with a fire burning in the fireplace. The stone walls were covered with wool hangings, and on the floor were thick, cosy rugs in bright jewel colours. Beside the fireplace was a big sofa; next to it stood a table covered with books and embroidery; and at the back of the room was a four-poster bed with silk hangings and fine wool blankets.

'Oh, Judith, what a lovely room,' said Grace. As she compared this marvellous chamber to her bare cold room at Drumshee, she could feel tears starting to her eyes again. She fought them down. She needed to think, and think clearly. It was essential that she should tell her story well, and that Brendan Davoren should believe her: he was her only chance of salvation.

Sitting on the sofa between Brendan and Judith,

with her eyes fixed on the flickering fire, Grace told them the whole story of her life: of the neglect and the cruelty, of the rumours that her uncle was selling her land, of the isolation in which she lived, and then of William Thompson and his plan to have her marry his son. When she came to the story of that terrible night and how she had woken up to find herself bound and gagged, Grace had to struggle very hard to keep from breaking down and crying. As she looked around that wonderful room, glowing with warmth and colour and love, it seemed almost impossible to describe the whitewashed chamber, the humpbacked shadows on the wall, and the stifling terror. Grace took Enda's advice and said nothing of the girl from the past — she gave them to understand that she had cut the rope on the protruding stone — but the story still sounded, even to her own ears, like some imaginary tale of horror.

Grace need not have worried about being believed, however. By the time she had finished, Judith was in tears, and her father was blowing his nose and trying to contain his anger.

'By God,' he swore, 'I'll see that the Fitzgeralds pay for this!'

Grace looked at him warily. All through her life, Grace had learned the hard lesson that she could rely only on herself.

I hope you can do something for me, she thought a little cynically; but I suppose the Fitzgeralds are my legal guardians, and maybe I'll have to go back to them eventually.

Grace shivered at the thought. Judith, noticing this, quickly dried her tears and became her practical self.

'Grace is tired out, Father,' she said. 'Let's leave all this until the morning. She can sleep here on the sofa.'

In ten minutes, everything was arranged. Dressed in one of Judith's silk nightgowns and wrapped in warm blankets, Grace stretched out on the sofa in front of the fire. Comfortable though she was, her mind was too active to go to sleep. She lay there, looking at the painted ceiling and wondering what she should do if her aunt and uncle insisted on taking her back to Drumshee. She could hear the distant roar of the sea, and she remembered the ship she had seen tossing at anchor .

If only I were a boy, she thought, I'd slip out and hide in that ship and sail away to England or Spain — except I couldn't leave Golden Dawn ....

An hour later, a glimmer of dawn began to show through the heavy velvet curtains. Tired of the thoughts that were going around and around in her head, Grace slipped off the sofa and went to the window. It was going to be a fine morning; already the sky was bright in the east, and the leaves on the beech trees outside the castle shone yellow and brown in the sun's first rays. Below the castle walls a wide river flowed down to a sandy beach and into the sea.

Grace turned and went back to the fireside, feeling a little more cheerful despite herself.

I wonder if I could go for a ride, she thought, and began to dress herself in Enda's breeches and jerkin. She was just putting on her shoes when Judith awoke and sat up in bed.

'Awake so early, Cousin?' she said with a smile.

The smile faded into an expression of slight horror as she added quickly, 'Oh, no, you mustn't wear those boy's clothes! Let me find you something pretty.'

Jumping out of bed, Judith hurried across the floor to a carved chest. Out of it she pulled dresses, more dresses than Grace had ever owned in her life.

'See,' she said, 'these are the gowns I've grown out of. Let's see which one is the prettiest.'

With all the excitement of a little girl with a new doll, Judith took up dress after dress and held them up against Grace. Each one looked almost brand new and smelled delicately of the lavender-flowers which had lain between the folds of the material.

'This primrose yellow would look good with your hazel eyes and your brown hair,' she said, with her head on one side; 'but no, I think it makes you look too young. What about this rose pink? It would suit you, but I think it may be too much of a party dress.'

She rummaged in the chest again, and, with a cry of triumph, took out a black velvet gown.

'Now this I know will suit you! You have such lovely rosy cheeks.'

Grace tried on the black velvet, but Judith was not satisfied. She shook her head firmly.

'No,' she said, 'you aren't big enough for it.'

She paused and looked at Grace sternly.

'You're very small for thirteen,' she said in a worried way. 'Grace, tell me the truth. Did Mary Fitzgerald give you enough to eat?'

'Oh yes,' Grace said, 'I had plenty to eat.'

A thought struck her, and she added slowly, 'I think my mother was small.'

Yes, Grace thought, as the memory began to clear in her mind. Yes, her mother had been small — small and pretty, with large hazel-green eyes and curly brown hair. Where is she now? Grace wondered. Deirdre always said that her mother was in heaven and looking down on her; if that was true, then her mother must be very sad to see the terrible danger her daughter was in .... At that thought Grace started to cry again. Judith took her in her arms, almost as if she were a mother herself, and kissed and petted her until Grace stopped sobbing.

'Come now,' Judith said gently, 'let me bathe your eyes with lavender water. There, that's better .... And I think this gown will suit you best.'

The gown Judith had chosen had a pale mauve silk underskirt and bodice, with a dark purple velvet overskirt. Placing Grace in front of the looking-glass, Judith brushed her curly brown hair and tied a purple velvet ribbon around it.

'There!' she said. 'Now you look lovely. Sit by the fire and look at this book while I get myself ready. It's a beautiful book; it has just arrived by ship from England.'

It was just eight o'clock when the two of them, hand in hand, walked into the dining hall. Just barely eight o'clock in the morning, but already there were voices from within. Grace closed the door behind herself and her cousin and turned towards the table; but she stopped abruptly, with her mouth dry and her knees buckling, as she looked straight into the angry faces of her aunt and uncle.

CHAPTER TEN

People who knew Brendan Davoren well always said that he was at his most dangerous when he was most polite. However, at that stage, Grace did not know Brendan Davoren very well, and her heart failed her when she saw his silken politeness to the Fitzgeralds and the courtliness with which he ushered them to table. Judith played her part as hostess, but her eyes were uneasy every time she looked at Grace.

The Fitzgeralds made several attempts to talk about Grace, but each time Brendan refused to listen: he diverted the talk into light remarks about the weather and about the latest news from Queen Elizabeth's court. He made a hearty breakfast, and pressed the Fitzgeralds to do likewise.

Grace ate nothing. She was numb with misery, like a trapped animal. She was just wondering whether she could escape from the room, put on her breeches and ride away from these people who had betrayed her, when Brendan spoke.

'Well, if everyone has finished, I think we'll go to my library. Judith, you come too; your cousin Grace will be glad of your company.'

Judith caught Grace's hand and squeezed it, but Grace made no response; she passively allowed herself to be led into the library. It was a beautiful room, lined from floor to ceiling with books bound in gold and red and green, and furnished with comfortable leather chairs and sofas. Brendan seated himself at a polished oaken desk and waved his visitors to two chairs. Judith sat on the sofa, keeping Grace by her side.

Mary Fitzgerald did not hesitate. Seeing Brendan Davoren's welcoming attitude, she had jumped to the conclusion that whatever story Grace had told, it had not been believed. As soon as everyone was seated, she plunged into speech.

'I thank you, Cousin, for sheltering this niece of mine,' she said. 'She has given us much trouble and worry during the past six years, ever since my poor brother and his wife died, but this last adventure has been the worst of all. We told her last night that she would have to stay in her chamber for the day unless she would mend her manners — and what did she do but escape from the castle through the cellar and ride over here to you! You can imagine how distraught we were when we found that she was missing.'

'I can imagine,' said Brendan softly.

There was a long silence. Grace knew that she should contradict her aunt, should plead with her cousin; but she did nothing, said nothing, just sat there in utter weariness and despair. The Fitzgeralds looked at her with hope rising in their eyes. They had thought it might be difficult to convince Brendan Davoren of the truth of their story, but this was proving easier than they could have imagined.

'Come then, niece,' continued Mary Fitzgerald, rising to her feet and holding out her hand to Grace. 'Make your apologies to your father's cousin for disturbing his household, and let us be going.' She crossed the room to Grace, who shrank against Judith's shoulder.

'No!' said Brendan Davoren.

Only one short word, but it cut through the tense air like a whiplash. Mary Fitzgerald stopped as if she had been struck; John got to his feet and moved to his wife. He stood there, ready for battle, with menace in every inch of his bull-like body. Mary put a restraining hand on his arm; her voice, light and unconcerned, belied the cold malice in her eyes.

'Oh, I fear we must take her now, Cousin. In your kindness, you may wish to keep her for a little holiday, but I must insist Grace comes with us. Such bad behaviour as she has shown should not go unpunished.'

Brendan rose to his feet, walked across the room, opened the door and bowed.

'Madam,' he said, 'I would not give a dog into your care, much less this frightened child.

'Robert,' he called. 'Robert, my cousins are returning to Drumshee. See them to their carriage, please.'

The Fitzgeralds could recognise iron purpose when they saw it. Without a glance at Grace, they walked slowly past him to the door of the castle. John turned with an angry scowl.

'You're wrong about one thing, Brendan Davoren,' he growled. 'We're not returning to Drumshee. We're going to Ennis to pick up a platoon of soldiers. We are the legal guardians of that girl, and the law will uphold our rights over her. I would advise you not to resist, or this fine castle of yours will lie in ruins before the day is over.'

When the door had closed behind them, Grace went over to Brendan.

'Thank you, Cousin,' she said, trying to sound brave, 'but you mustn't risk your castle and your life and Judith's life for me. Let me take Golden Dawn and go. Enda will find me a hiding place. There are old ruined houses near the bog; I can live in one of them, and Enda will bring me food. In January my uncle and aunt are going to London, to Queen Elizabeth's court, and then I can live with Bridget and Enda.'

Brendan laughed gently and drew her onto his lap, as if she were a small child.

'She may not be very big, Judith,' he said with amusement, 'but she has the courage of a lion. But now, my dears, we must think and plan. You say, Grace, that your uncle and aunt are going to London in January. Well, we've also planned to go to London. That ship you've seen in the bay is to take us there next week.'

Grace looked at him with hope dawning in her eyes. He gave her a reassuring pat on the hand, before turning to Judith. 'What do you say, my dear? Could you be ready today? Don't worry about your finery. We can buy all you need in London, and all of it will be in the latest fashion. What say you?'

Judith's eyes were shining. 'Oh, Father, does this mean Grace will come to London with us? Oh, certainly, I can be ready. Give me an hour and everything will be packed.'

'Well, in that case,' said Brendan, 'I'll walk down to the harbour and talk to the master of the ship. He told me yesterday that he could go at an hour's notice. It will take that pair of villains three hours to get to Ennis. We'll see no soldiers here before evening —

and by then,' he added cheerfully, giving Grace a warm hug, 'this little bird will have flown away across the sea. Come with me, my dear; we'll leave Judith to her household cares, and you shall walk to the harbour with me.'

Grace got to her feet, hope beginning to warm within her. She turned a face of incredulous joy towards her cousin — but then a sudden thought struck her, and her face clouded over again. 'Oh, Cousin Brendan,' she said, 'I can't leave Golden Dawn. He'd be miserable without me.'

Brendan laughed. 'Don't worry, my dear,' he said. 'We'll only be gone for a few months. Remember, this was your Golden Dawn's first home. Robert was the one who trained him when he was a foal, and Robert's daughter, who's about your size, will be delighted to exercise him.'

With that Grace had to be content. She knew from Golden Dawn's gentle nature and soft mouth that he had been treated well when he was young, so she was sure Robert could be trusted to care for him. With a happy heart, she prepared for the walk.

Wrapped in one of Judith's warm cloaks, Grace walked with her cousin beside the shining river and up the narrow cobbled street which led to the little harbour of Liscannor. Grace had never seen the sea before, and everything about it was magical to her: the blue immensity of the ocean, the white-capped waves, the smell of salt, the crying of the seabirds — and, best of all, the ship rocking gently on the green water, with its great sails cracking in the wind.

CHAPTER ELEVEN

It was early in the month of December 1587 when the little ship eventually arrived in London. It had been a difficult and sometimes dangerous journey. The weather had been stormy, and the English Channel was full of ships; the great Spanish fleet, the Armada, was trying to attack England, but the English were holding the Spanish troops at bay in the Netherlands. Grace, however, had enjoyed every minute of the voyage. She had never once been seasick, and she had never felt worried. And at last they had arrived safely.

London seemed very strange and wonderful to the two girls, as they leaned over the side of the ship and watched its slow progress up the River Thames. The streets were lined with great stone houses, and everywhere they looked they could see crowds of beautifully-dressed ladies and gentlemen coming in and out of the houses, or entering their coaches, or stopping to talk on the pavements.

'Grace,' said Judith, 'Grace, this might be my home in the future. I know my father would like me to marry an English nobleman.'

'Would you like that?' asked Grace curiously.

'Only if he's very rich and handsome,' laughed Judith.

'No, but would you like to leave Ireland?' Grace persisted.

'Well,' said Judith seriously, 'Father's afraid there

may be very difficult and dangerous times coming to Ireland, and he thinks I'd be safer in England.'

'I think I'd miss Ireland, if I were away for too long,' said Grace. She suddenly thought of Enda, and wondered what he was doing this morning.

Judith looked at her in a troubled way.

'Did you like that Robert Thompson from Inchovea Castle, Grace?' she enquired.

'Oh, no,' said Grace with a giggle. 'You should have seen him. He was so fat and pasty-faced! That's one Englishman I won't marry. In any case, I think I'll be too young to go to court. I'm not yet fourteen.'

'Lady Mary Sidney was only about your age when she came to court, and she was married within a few months. You wait and see — by this time next year, we'll both be old married ladies! But in the meantime, let's have as much fun as we can.'

They did have a splendid time in London. This was the first time Grace had ever had another girl for a friend, and she soon began to enjoy all the fun of choosing new clothes, going to parties, discussing young men and giggling over silly jokes. Brendan Davoren was very rich, and ever since his wife had died he had dedicated his whole life to making his daughter happy. He could never refuse her anything. And he was determined to give Grace a happy time before her aunt and uncle arrived in London. The house which he had rented seemed to be filled with merchants bringing lengths of silk and velvet and brocade, and sewing-women were stitching busily all day long.

At last the great day arrived when Grace and Judith

were to be presented to Queen Elizabeth herself. Brendan had already met her: like all the Irish chieftains, he had been required to make a ceremonial surrender of his land to the Queen, and had had three-quarters of it granted back to him. He had told the Queen about his daughter Judith, and of his hopes and plans for her, and he had also told her Grace's story. The Queen, he reported, had been most interested in the fact that Grace had four thousand acres of land.

'You'll have a private audience with Her Majesty,' Brendan told the girls, 'and afterwards you are to attend a great entertainment at the palace. There will be music and dancing, so you must wear your most beautiful clothes. '

Neither Grace nor Judith slept much the night before the presentation, and they were trembling with excitement as they prepared to leave for the palace. Judith wore a gown of black velvet, whose bodice and overskirt were sewn with hundreds of tiny pearls. Her long golden hair, held back from her forehead by a black velvet band, rippled down her back.

'Oh, Judith, you look beautiful,' gasped Grace.

'And so do you — you look exquisite,' said Judith generously.

Grace looked down at her own gown. Yes, she thought with satisfaction, it's absolutely exquisite. She was dressed in a farthingale of deep rose-pink velvet, and a cream silk kirtle embroidered with pale pink roses. Around her neck, as always, was the gold necklace she had found in the cellar at Drumshee.

'You look like a beautiful little rose,' said Judith,

surveying her up and down. 'All the noblemen at court will be asking for your hand.'

'Not all,' laughed Grace. 'Lord Berkeley will only have eyes for you, as usual.'

Judith blushed, but just then her father arrived to escort them to the waiting carriage, so she said no more.

When they arrived at the palace, they took their places in the antechamber and waited for the Queen to appear. After about an hour, a ripple of excitement ran through the crowd. Grace was so small that she could not see the Queen, but luckily there was a small footstool just behind her; so, with a hand on Judith's arm to steady herself, she hopped up on the stool and had her first glimpse of the famous Queen Elizabeth of England.

'Oh,' she gasped in Judith's ear, 'she's wearing a wig! And her teeth are quite black — and look at her face! It's all covered with thick white paint. I thought she was supposed to be very beautiful!'

'Hush!' murmured Judith. 'Come down, Grace.'

Grace saw the Queen turn towards her, and she got down hastily. 'Be on your guard with the Queen,' Brendan had told her the day before. 'She doesn't like the Irish; she thinks they bring nothing but problems — and you're certainly going to be a problem to her. She's heard about you from the Fitzgeralds, and she'll have to make up her mind about who is telling the truth.'

Grace was certain that the Queen could not have heard her; but there was no doubt that, when it came to their turn to be presented, Queen Elizabeth looked at Grace coldly.

'Well, Mistress Grace,' said the Queen abruptly, 'what is this I hear about you running away from those good people, your Aunt and Uncle Fitzgerald?'

A few months before, Grace would have said nothing in reply to this, but the last months of being petted and praised had given her back the courage she had had as a child. A great wave of anger rose inside her. She felt her cheeks burn, and all Brendan Davoren's words of caution were swept out of her head.

'They were not good people, Your Majesty,' she said in loud clear tones. 'They did their best to murder me.'

There was a sudden and complete silence in the room. The murmuring voices of the courtiers ceased, and Grace felt every eye in the room was upon her.

Queen Elizabeth raised her delicate eyebrows so far that the white paint on her high forehead seemed to be in danger of cracking. With a look of deep disapproval, she turned from Grace to Judith.

'I see that reports have not exaggerated your beauty,' she said graciously to Judith. 'Do you like England?'

'Oh, I love England,' said Judith. 'I could live here for ever. The only thing I miss is riding my horse every day.'

The Queen's sombre expression lightened.

'Well said,' she exclaimed. 'I hear that you are an excellent rider, like all Irishwomen. Tomorrow morning, you and your cousin shall ride with me and the young people of the court.' She smiled graciously.

Judith nudged Grace, and they curtseyed and withdrew, walking backwards, as they had been told they must in the Queen's presence.

'Oh, Grace, how could you?' said Judith in horrified tones, once they were outside the door.

Grace blushed with embarrassment. She was still quite angry inside, but she knew she had been stupid.

'Don't tell your father,' she implored.

'No, of course not. Anyway, you'll have another chance tomorrow, when we go out riding with the Queen. Now forget it, and let's have fun this evening!'

They did have fun. In fact, Grace had never had such fun in her life as she had that evening. For once, she was grateful that her aunt had made her practise dancing every day. Courtier after courtier came forward to lead her out in the dance. In the looking-glasses set all around the room, she could see that her cheeks were the same colour as the velvet of her dress; her hair clung in damp clusters around her forehead, and her eyes were like stars.

Just before suppertime, Judith ran up and seized Grace by the hand.

'Oh, Grace, I'm so happy!' she whispered. 'Lord Berkeley has asked me to be his wife, and the Queen and my father have agreed.'

Grace kissed her cousin lovingly, but with a trace of sadness. For the first time in six years, she had begun to feel that she was part of a family; and now the family was about to break up.

Judith, reading her thoughts, tried to console her.

'Grace, I'm sure a match will be made for you, too. Everyone's talking about you, and I've heard that the

Queen wants you to marry an English nobleman as well.'

Grace laughed. But throughout the rest of the evening, while candles flickered in golden sconces and women and men dressed in silks and velvets circled round and around the floor in a glorious medley of colours — amid all this splendour, she had just one picture in her mind. It was the picture of a misty green Irish hillside, a golden pony with his mane blowing in the Atlantic breeze, and a tall boy on an old farm horse riding by her side.

CHAPTER TWELVE

Brendan Davoren was up at dawn the next morning, determined to find a pair of horses which would be worthy of the girls when they went riding with the Queen. He was delighted by the Queen's remark about Irishwomen being good at horseback riding, and he wanted to show just how good both Judith and Grace were.

It was almost midday when he came back, and the girls were waiting impatiently for him outside the house. It was a beautiful winter's morning, and the sun showed golden in the smoky London sky.

'No matter what horse your father finds for me, Judith,' Grace said, 'it will never be like Golden Dawn.'

At that moment Brendan came trotting down the street on his shining chestnut stallion, leading a beautiful milk-white mare. Judith, with a gasp of admiration, ran down the steps and began to stroke the mare's graceful arched neck. Grace, however, could only stand there, unable to move; for around the corner came a stable-boy leading a young pony which was as golden and blond as Golden Dawn himself.

'She's for you, Grace,' said Brendan, his face full of pleasure at her delight. 'She's very young and hasn't been completely schooled yet, but as soon as I saw her I knew she'd be a perfect mate for Golden Dawn. Be careful with her, though — she's young and full of energy, and at the moment she's a bit wild. You won't find her as easy as Golden Dawn.'

In a moment, Grace was up on the pony and taking the reins from the stable-boy. She trotted her new golden pony up the London street. The pony shied when a housemaid threw a pail of dirty water out of a window, but Grace patted her neck and spoke to her soothingly, and after a minute she trotted on quite happily. When Grace reached the top of the street she turned and rode back, stopping with perfect control just in front of the steps.

'Well done,' said Brendan.

The stable-boy nodded admiringly. 'She can manage her, sir,' he said happily.

'Oh, Grace, what will you call her?' asked Judith.

Grace looked up at the sun shining overhead and said, 'I think I'll call her Golden Noon. That will go well with Golden Dawn.'

Judith nodded in approval. 'I think I'll call my horse Moonlight,' she said.

'Now remember, Grace,' said Brendan, 'do your best riding for the Queen. She always thinks more highly of people who are good riders. She admires courage more than anything else; and we don't want her to think that on that night at Drumshee you were just a little girl frightened by a nightmare.'

'I'll do my best,' said Grace, thinking that it would be easier to jump over the highest wall than to please the Queen.

By the time they arrived at the Royal Park, most people were already waiting, seated on their horses. The Queen arrived shortly afterwards, accompanied by Lord Leicester, her Master of Horse. She smiled graciously at Judith, but only gave Grace a cool nod.

Oh dear, thought Grace; I'd better do some

spectacular riding. I think it will take a lot to change her opinion of me.

Judith immediately moved to ride beside Lord Berkeley, and Grace found herself placed beside Lord Montague. He was a boy of seventeen, the eldest son

of an earl, and she had danced with him many times the evening before. Now, in the cold light of the afternoon, Grace thought he looked silly and girlish. His red velvet breeches — slashed to show their white silk lining — were too showy, and it was obvious that he was not a good horseman: his beautiful iron-grey stallion reared up on its hind legs and danced with terror at the slightest provocation. Grace glanced at him in surprise and thought how much

Enda would have loved to ride a horse like that.

But soon she forgot Lord Montague and settled down to a hard gallop. Golden Noon was indeed very lively, and Grace decided that giving her her

head for a while would make her easier to handle afterwards. She wished that young Lord Montague would stop trying to keep up with her. It was obvious that he had little control over his horse.

After about ten minutes Golden Noon began to calm down, and Grace found that she was enjoying riding her. The young pony was not as responsive as Golden Dawn, but Grace knew that the kind of relationship she had with Golden Dawn could only be built up over months of riding.

Now that they were going more steadily, Grace could look around. She found that many of the courtiers, including the Queen and the Earl of Leicester, were watching her with interest and admiration.

Ahead of them was a high gate leading to the forest. A servant boy was standing nearby, ready to open it if the party wished to ride in the forest.

Here's my chance, thought Grace. Turning Golden Noon towards the gate and whispering words of encouragement into her ear, she sailed over the gate with several inches to spare.

A sigh of astonishment came from the onlookers — but it turned to a gasp of horror as Lord Montague's horse, trying to follow, struck the gate with his leg. Completely out of control, with his fetlock bleeding badly, the maddened horse bolted into the forest. The unfortunate boy on his back screamed wildly.

As soon as Grace realised what was happening, she pulled her horse around and galloped off after them. She realised that the young lord must soon be swept off the horse's back by the overhanging branches, so she rode Golden Noon in a wide circle, doing her best to get ahead. But the grey horse was galloping at full speed, and Grace began to doubt whether she would be able to cut him off.

'Come on, Golden Noon!' she whispered.

The pony gathered herself up, made a supreme effort and sped past the grey. Hauling on the reins, Grace turned Golden Noon to the left, forcing Lord Montague's horse to turn as well. With the two horses galloping side by side, Grace leant over and managed to grasp the bridle of the grey horse. Gradually, little by little, she slowed him down.

Trotting sedately, they rejoined the company waiting by the gate. Lord Montague was not injured, but his fine new doublet was ruined and his handsome, girlish face was marred by scratches and tears. Grace was feeling rather pleased with herself — but the Queen did not look happy.

'How now, Mistress!' she said sharply. 'We want none of your wayward ways here.'

No one asked him to follow me, thought Grace; but this time she had the wisdom to keep her thoughts to herself.

'But what wonderful riding, and what a lovely colour in her cheeks! She looks like a little rose,' laughed the Earl of Leicester.

'Methinks, my lord, that it is a wild Irish rose,' said the Queen tartly. She rode on without another glance at Grace.

Judith rode up and joined Grace. She smiled protectively, but Grace knew that her cousin was worried. There was no chance now that the Queen would take a fancy to Grace.

She was right. The Fitzgeralds arrived at the court the following week, and Grace and Brendan Davoren were summoned to the palace to make their case before the Queen.

Grace told her story badly. During the past happy months she had seldom allowed thoughts of that terrible night to enter her head, and now it all seemed like a bad dream. As she faltered through her recital, Grace herself almost began to wonder whether it was true.

The shocked faces of her aunt and uncle, and the cool glance of the Queen, made her more and more confused. Finally she fell silent, her cheeks flushing a deep red and her eyes fixed on the floor, the very picture of guilt.

The Fitzgeralds, by contrast, told their story well. They admitted that they might have been over-strict with Grace — perhaps they had made her study for too many hours — but they had found her so wild that they wished to teach her discipline. At the word 'wild' Grace stole a glance at the Queen and saw her nod to herself in agreement.

Brendan did his best for Grace, but it was clear that the Queen was hardly listening. Only when he spoke of the rumours that John Fitzgerald was selling off Grace's land did the Queen show any interest. Money and property were always of interest to Queen Elizabeth, and she knew of many cases where guardians had abused their trust. It looked as if Her Majesty did believe at least this one part of the story.

When Brendan had finished speaking, there was a long silence. John and Mary Fitzgerald held their breath. Either they had won the battle — or they were ruined and disgraced for ever.

Finally the Queen gave her judgement. Grace would remain in London, in Brendan Davoren's care, until the month of June. If by that time she was neither married nor betrothed to an Englishman, she would have to return to Ireland with John and Mary Fitzgerald. Within one month of their arrival back in Ireland, or of Grace's betrothal, the Fitzgeralds would have to render up an account of their stewardship of Grace Barry's property. And if land had indeed been sold, they would have to either buy it back or repay the money.

CHAPTER THIRTEEN

Grace did not marry within the five months, nor was she betrothed. The Queen's words about her had gone around the court: where once everyone had thought of her as 'that pretty little Irish girl', now Grace was known as 'that wild little Irish rose'. The Fitzgeralds spread the rumour that Grace was accustomed to gallop around the countryside at night with a farm lad, and not even the thought of four thousand acres could make the fathers of young nobles look on her with favour.

In some ways Grace did not really mind. She did not want to marry any of those young men; when she compared them to Enda, none of them seemed worth much. Grace enjoyed the parties and the dancing, the pretty gowns and the fine food, but she was happiest of all when she was riding her beautiful Golden Noon through the parks and forests.

In the middle of May, on a day of glorious sunshine, Judith was married to Lord Berkeley. Soon after this, Brendan Davoren made a last effort to persuade the Queen to transfer Grace's guardianship to him.

Grace dressed herself with great care for the important interview. She wore a grey dress, but when she looked at herself in the mirror she felt dissatisfied with her appearance. She thought she looked colourless and insignificant.

'The trouble is,' she said to Brendan in the carriage, 'I don't really know what sort of person to be with

Queen Elizabeth. People say she likes you to be bold and courageous and to speak your mind, but that certainly didn't work for me.'

'Well, my dear, cleverer people than you or I have puzzled for years over that problem. The fact is that it's very difficult to know what way the Queen will think. It might be better not to say too much about the attempted murder this time. Concentrate on the land issue; that seemed to interest her more, last time. She won't want the Fitzgeralds feathering their nest with your acres. She'd prefer you to marry an Englishman and hand your property over to him.'

Grace said nothing. She knew that Brendan too would like her to marry in England, but she did not want to. She wanted to get back to Ireland. She had never mentioned Enda to Brendan — he would have been shocked — but certainly Enda was part of the reason why she wanted to return home, and why she could not imagine marrying an Englishman.

The court was crowded when they came in; everyone was interested in this case. The Queen, however, decided to hear the case in private. She sat with her chin in her hand, gazing coldly at Grace, while Brendan went over the facts again.

It was a fruitless afternoon. The Queen was determined to hand Grace back to her guardians. She made only two concessions: she announced that she would require regular reports of Grace's health and happiness from the County Sheriff of Clare; and she decided that if it was proved that land had been sold, the Fitzgeralds would have to come back to London to stand trial and make restitution. With that Brendan had to be content.

Grace, too, had to be content. At least, she thought, now it would be much more difficult for the Fitzgeralds to get rid of me. There are far too many people looking suspiciously at them, and there would be no hope of disguising my death as an accident.

'Would there be any chance of coming to some arrangement with them?' wondered Grace to Judith, shortly before her return to Ireland. 'I don't care how much land they sold, as long as I can live safely and happily. I could give them enough money to live in Galway, and I could live at Drumshee.'

'Oh, Grace, you mustn't say anything of the sort to them. Father says you're in no danger from them now. They won't dare do anything to you. You must keep your land for your children.'

Grace smiled to herself. Judith did make her laugh — she always sounded so elderly! She was bustling around the room, taking dress after dress out of the tall presses.

'Grace, we must pack these dresses really well, so they'll be in no danger from seawater or moths.'

'There's no point in taking them,' said Grace drearily. 'I'll never get any opportunity to wear them.'

'Nonsense,' said Judith. 'You'll see, things will be different now. Why, the Fitzgeralds might be quite anxious to get you married, if they dislike you as much as you say. They'll probably arrange all sorts of entertainments for you when you go back.'

Grace said nothing. There did not seem much point in saying anything. After all, by now the murder attempt did not seem too real even to her; it was not surprising that Judith had almost forgotten about it.

At that moment, there was a knock on the door and two footmen struggled in with a large chest, beautifully carved. Behind them came Brendan Davoren.

'That's just a little present for you, my dear,' he said to Grace. 'Judith tells me that you need somewhere to keep your finery. When everything is packed, we'll seal it with wax; then your things will keep for a few hundred years.'

Judith laughed, but Grace thought gloomily that they would probably not be worn for a few hundred years. However, she cheered up when they took all the dresses out and spread them on the bed and over chairs. They were so beautiful !

One by one the gowns were put into the chest: purple velvet, green silk, royal blue satin, white brocade trimmed with crimson; and on top of them all, the cream silk kirtle embroidered with pale pink roses, with its farthingale of deep rose velvet, which Grace had worn that night at Queen Elizabeth's court.

'Grace, what about Golden Noon?' asked Brendan, a week before Grace was due to sail. 'She's yours, you know. Would you like to take her with you, or shall I bring her when I come over next spring?'

Grace had been thinking about this for the last few weeks; she had known she would have to decide.

'I hate parting from Golden Noon,' she said thoughtfully, 'but I really don't know what will happen when I get back to Drumshee. The Fitzgeralds may not be willing to make proper arrangements for her on the ship, and I couldn't bear to see her suffer. No, if you don't mind, I think it would be best if you brought her over in the spring. I won't worry about her while you have her.'

In the end, their voyage was delayed until the end of August. After months of waiting, the great Armada from Spain had finally arrived. A fierce battle was fought in the English Channel, near Dover; fireships were launched at the great Spanish galleons, and the English managed to defeat the Armada before the Spanish reinforcements could arrive from the Netherlands. The Spanish ships were driven into the North Sea and left to make their way back to Spain by the northern route.

The Fitzgeralds judged that it was safe to leave England. They decided to return to Ireland by the southern route, by Devon and Cornwall and then along the south coast of Ireland.

The sea voyage passed quietly. Grace saw almost nothing of her aunt, as Mary Fitzgerald suffered badly from seasickness and kept to her cabin for most of the days. Her husband John paced the deck of the *Seagull* every day, his distress of mind showing clearly in his restless body. He said nothing to Grace — indeed, he hardly seemed to see her. Knitting his brows and feverishly counting and recounting on his fingers, he seemed to be continually trying to work out some sum. The result never seemed to satisfy him. At the end of his calculations he would turn to the railings of the ship, with a groan of despair or a muttered curse, and stare down at the green waves as if wondering whether to end his troubles by casting himself overboard.

As Grace stood on deck, leaning against the mast and watching her uncle, she understood that matters were far more serious than anyone had imagined. Possibly even Mary Fitzgerald did not realise how much land had been sold; but Grace knew that no man would be in such depths of despair for the sake of a couple of hundred acres. She wondered how he had managed to spend all the money; the Fitzgeralds did not live extravagantly. And then, in a flash, she remembered the words she had overheard Deirdre saying, so long ago.

'That John Fitzgerald!' she had said. 'He's nothing but a wastrel and a gambler.'

That was probably the answer: he had lost the money gambling. But whatever he had done with it, now he was clearly very short of money. There was none of the staying overnight, or spending a few days in port, which Grace had enjoyed on her leisurely voyage to England with the Davorens. John Fitzgerald seemed determined to make the journey as quickly and as cheaply as possible.

But within a month of their arrival in Ireland, he would have to account for all Grace's property. Between himself and ruin stood one small life; and looking at his dark face, Grace shivered and moved closer to the helmsman.

CHAPTER FOURTEEN

𝕴t was September of the year 1588 when the *Sea-gull* finally made its way up the rough and rocky west coast of Ireland. The weather had turned bad, and high winds and mountainous seas had several times driven the ship off course. It seemed to Grace as if they would never get to Drumshee. Her tension was so great that, although previously she had dreaded coming back to the castle, now she almost longed for it. One way or another, thought Grace, once we get back, I'll know what's going to happen to me.

One September morning, when Grace came up from her cabin, she could see that this was going to be one of the worst days of the voyage. The waves towered above the little ship like green mountains, and the west wind was so strong that she felt as if the breath was snatched from her lips. She clung to the top of the ladder leading from the cabins.

It was fortunate that she was holding tightly to the ladder: a moment later an enormous wave struck the side of the ship and it heeled over, with its great mast and sail almost in the water and the deck standing at a right angle. For a moment it seemed that nothing would right the ship, that there could be no escape from the watery trough in which it was lodged. Grace held on and looked down at the green valley beneath her. While one part of her mind was listening to the shouts of the sailors, who were desperately trying to haul the mast upright, another corner of her mind was saying quietly: So this is to be my grave, after all.

The next moment it was all over. With a terrible straining and creaking, the captain managed to turn the ship so that it drove through the centre of the wave. The deck was level again. Grace was drenched with cold salt water, but the danger had been averted for the moment.

The great sails filled out. They were in the shelter of the island of Inisheer, and the west wind was behind them, driving the ship towards the coast.

The ship was going fast, too fast. One minute Grace could just make out the bulk of the Cliffs of Moher, far in the distance; the next minute they were looming above her. If the ship continued to go at this pace, there would be no saving it from destruction on the jagged rocks. There's no beach here, thought Grace, no gentle strand where a ship might land without harm; only the cruel rocks and the driving sea.

However, the captain knew the coast well. At the last moment, when it seemed that the ship must be lost, the sails were hauled around and the prow was turned to the north. Perhaps he'll head for Galway Bay, thought Grace.

She could no longer see anything. The ship was churning through the water, sending up such clouds of dense spray that it was like moving in a white cloud. Her eyes burned from the salt spray; she longed to wipe them, but dared not release her grip on the rope. She blinked rapidly several times — and then opened her eyes wide in horror. Far above them loomed a dark shape. For one terrible moment, Grace thought that the ship must have swung around again and be driving straight at the rocky cliffs once more.

At that moment everyone else on deck saw the shape too. Shouts of 'Ship ahoy!' rang out.

'My God!' shouted the captain. 'It's one of the Armada galleons! It must have gone astray in the storm.'

The Spanish ship was a huge vessel, but it was helpless in the tempest. Unlike the small Irish boat, it was unable to turn and twist and ride the waves. Grace watched in horror as another mighty gust of wind drove a gigantic wave against its side. A moment later, the great ship was driven onto the rocks of a small island and smashed into a thousand pieces.

The *Seagull*, too, was in trouble again. The wave which had destroyed the Spanish ship had swung the prow of the *Seagull* around towards the west again, and again she plunged down into the depths of a trough. Her decks were swept with icy salt water, and Grace could see nothing but a hail of white spray. She held her breath — but once more the brave little ship righted itself.

And now they were in the calmer water on the lee side of the island, and before them was the little village of Fisherstreet. The wind dropped a little, and the crew breathed sighs of relief and turned to look at the Spanish galleon.

Planks and pieces of masts floated on the white-topped waves, but there was no sign of any living man. The ship had broken up so violently and so quickly that it appeared that none of the Spaniards had been able to save themselves. After scanning the sea for several minutes, the captain gave the order to turn the *Seagull* into the port of Fisherstreet.

At that moment, Grace's eye was caught by a flash of gold in the water. She shouted as loudly as she could, and pointed. Clinging to one of the floating spars was a man; and faintly, on the wind, they could hear his voice crying for help.

The captain manoeuvred his ship as near as he dared. Tying a noose in a rope, he flung it towards the unfortunate man. It fell short. He tried again; again it fell out of the man's reach.

The wind had begun to rise again. The waves began to batter the floating pieces of wood, knocking them against the man who clung to the spar.

The captain crossed himself and said, 'In the name of God, may I reach him this time. If I don't, he'll go to the bottom of the sea, like all the rest of them.'

He whirled the noose around his head and flung it with all his strength. It fell several feet short — but at that moment a wave lifted the man and drove him forward, just far enough to allow him to grasp the noose. Paddling the water with one hand, he managed to pass the noose over his head with the other; then he slipped both arms inside it, so that the noose was around his chest and he could be drawn towards the *Seagull*.

He climbed swiftly up the rope ladder which had been let down for him, reaching the deck just as John and Mary Fitzgerald came up from below.

The figure that met their eyes was a very splendid one. The Spaniard wore a doublet of purple silk, trimmed with a gold silk collar; down the front of his doublet ran a line of gold buttons, and around his neck was a gold cross. He was clearly a man of wealth and importance. But John Fitzgerald was not impressed.

'By heaven, Captain, are you mad?' he swore. 'The sheriff will burn my ship and throw us in prison if he finds out we've rescued one of the Queen's enemies from the Armada! You'd do best to throw him overboard and have done with it. Or else,' he added with his sneering laugh, 'you can just hang him, as you have a noose ready around his neck.'

The Spaniard obviously understood English, for he turned immediately to John Fitzgerald .

'Señor,' he said, 'I beg of you, spare my life. My name is Don Octavio de Fuentes y Cabezada, and I am one of the richest men in Spain. If you can hide me for a few days, until the storm ends, and then lend me your ship and your valiant captain, I will send you from Spain any sum of money you may require.'

John laughed mirthlessly. 'Yes,' he said, 'I'll surely lend you my ship — and probably never see it again. What is there to make you keep your word, once you're back in Spain?'

Don Octavio's eyes flashed with anger, but he kept his temper well under control.

'Then come with me to Spain,' he said coolly. 'I will give you wealth beyond your wildest dreams. I will give you gold enough to purchase ten ships such as this, gold enough to buy ten thousand acres if ever you wish to return to Ireland again.'

There was a long silence. The two men stared at each other. Grace held her breath. She could see quite clearly what was going through her uncle's mind. If he could trust Don Octavio's word, this could be the answer to all his problems ....

'I'll do it,' he said abruptly.

He knew there was no other solution. In the past

few months, he had been over the situation again and again in his mind. And he knew that chance had suddenly presented him with a way to escape. John Fitzgerald was a gambler; he did not hesitate.

'I'll do it,' he repeated. 'You can come back to our castle at Drumshee for a few days, and then we'll set sail. You'll have to pay the captain and his men five hundred pounds of Spanish gold.'

'Agreed,' said Don Octavio with a courtly bow.

'Captain? '

The captain spoke for some time with his crew. Then he turned back to John Fitzgerald. 'Aye, aye, sir, we'll do it,' he said.

Mary Fitzgerald had been listening to all this with alarm — an alarm which was fast turning to terror.

'Don't do it, John!' she pleaded. 'The sheriff will burn the castle over our heads and throw us into prison. The risk is too great.'

Her husband drew her aside. He began to talk in a low rapid voice, and eventually she nodded her head resignedly.

'Captain, we'll leave all our chests on board the ship until we come back,' said John, turning from his wife to the captain. 'Will you hire us a coach to get us back to Drumshee as soon as we land? I'll lend our Spanish friend a cloak to hide his fine clothes. Then get the ship ready for the voyage; and as soon as the weather is right, send me word and we'll come. In the meantime,' he added in a low voice, 'keep your crew on board the ship with you, and let no man know what has happened here tonight. Report to the captain of the garrison that the galleon went down with all hands.'

CHAPTER FIFTEEN

$\mathbf{I}$t was the middle of the afternoon when the coach arrived at Drumshee. The Fitzgeralds immediately took Don Octavio into the little parlour at the side of the Great Hall. They had not spoken a word to Grace since leaving the ship, and she was glad to escape to her room. Her clothes were still soaking wet.

When Grace arrived in her chamber she looked around with a feeling of deep depression. Now that she had spent nearly a year living in fine comfortable rooms, this room seemed more like a prison cell than ever. Shivering violently, she pulled off her wet clothes and climbed into her bed. It was cold and damp, and as hard as stone. I'd forgotten how thin and rough the blankets are, she thought.

Grace did not sleep, but as she grew warmer her spirits began to rise. If the Fitzgeralds did go to Spain, they were unlikely to bother to take her with them. Once they had money from some other source she would be of no further use to them — and, even better, she would be no further threat to them. In Spain they would be safe from reprisals for selling her land.

As Grace's spirits rose, she started to make plans. She would stay in her room and pretend to be ill; if she stayed out of their way, they would probably forget all about her. And as soon as they were gone, she would go across the hills to Bridget and Enda and stay with them.

Now that she felt more cheerful, Grace began to feel hungry. She got out of bed and, pulling on a warm wrapper, stole down the spiral staircase. The voices continued from the parlour; she passed its closed door as silently as she could and went on down to the kitchen.

Deirdre was there. She took Grace in her arms, and tears of happiness ran down her face, while the rest of the kitchen maids and the little boy who cleaned the vegetables looked on with big smiles. There was one strange face there, an ugly boy of about nineteen, but Grace soon forgot about him. She sat on a low stool, in front of the blazing fire, and hungrily swallowed the soup which Deirdre had ladled out for her.

'I hear you brought back a Spaniard,' said Deirdre, sitting down beside her and getting ready for a good comfortable gossip.

Grace almost dropped her spoon with shock. Of course — she should have known: this was the country, and nothing is ever a secret there for long. But this was dangerous talk. She caught an expression of intense curiosity in the eyes of the strange boy.

'No,' she muttered. 'He's just a friend of Uncle's.'

Again she caught the stranger's eye, and she knew from his expression that he did not believe her.

Deirdre saw her troubled glance and fiercely ordered everyone about their business; and in the bustle, nobody noticed the strange boy slip through the outer door.

Only when the kitchen was empty did Deirdre speak again.

'Something's going on, pet,' she whispered. 'In the

last half hour your uncle has sent to all the farms for every man he can get, and William says he's taken twenty muskets from the gun room. I've been told to make a meal for the men, here in the kitchen; they'll all sleep here tonight.'

Grace thought this over, but there did not seem to be much she could do about it, so she tried to put it out of her mind.

'Is my governess still here, Deirdre?'

'No, she is not. Your aunt sent her away the day after you went. She was blamed for not keeping a proper eye on you.'

Grace finished her soup and bread and got to her feet .

'Deirdre,' she said, 'if my aunt asks for me, say that I'm tired and not very well, so I've gone to bed early.'

Grace went back up the stone staircase as quietly as she had come. It was true, she did feel tired: every bone in her body ached, and she hoped she was not going to be ill. She paused for a rest halfway up the stairs.

Looking out of the landing window, she saw the strange boy walking down the avenue. She wondered who he was, and why he was leaving the castle when all the workers were being brought indoors, but she was too tired to care much. As soon as she reached her chamber, she thankfully climbed back into her bed and fell sound asleep.

It was about ten o'clock when Grace woke up. She felt much better; she knew that she was clear-headed and had no trace of fever. She got out of bed and looked out of the window.

The west wind was still blowing strongly and it was a dark and cloudy night, but as she looked, the wind blew the clouds from the face of the moon for a moment; and on the road to Tullagh and Kilfenora, Grace saw a flash of silver. Once before, on a dark night last November, she had seen moonlight gleaming on silver like that. She knew instantly what it was: the soldiers were coming.

She turned away from the window and opened the chest at the bottom of her bed. Yes, Enda's old breeches and jerkin were still there. Quickly and with steady hands, she pulled them on, tucking her gold necklace inside the collar of the jerkin.

She would have to warn her uncle and aunt. Evil as they had been to her, she could not let them be killed in their beds.

Grace came out of her room — and stopped. There was no need for her to warn them. At every window there was a man with a musket, and already the heavy iron gates of the courtyard had been closed and enormous stones were being dragged into position behind them. In the shadow of the gate were more men with muskets. John Fitzgerald was taking no chances.

Grace went back to her window. It looked as if there were only about thirty soldiers on the road. It will be almost impossible for them to get into the castle, she thought. Whoever had built Drumshee Castle had built it to be defended. It was set on the very top of the hill, with a ditch all around it, and anyone approaching from any side would be seen instantly by the men at the windows.

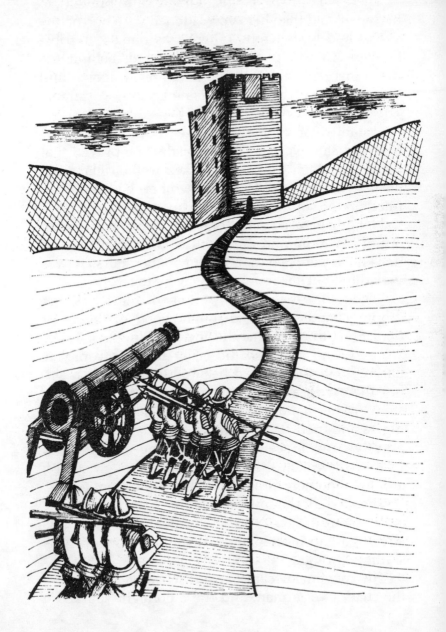

There's no real danger, Grace said bravely to herself — and then her eyes widened with horror.

She had been wrong. There was danger. Terrible danger. Around the bend in the road, behind the marching soldiers, came a large wagon; and mounted upon the wagon was a great iron cannon. The castle was doomed.

Instantly Grace made up her mind. There was only one safe way out of the castle. She prayed that the hole Golden Dawn had kicked in the cellar wall, on that terrible night last November, had not been filled up too solidly for her to reopen it ....

Nobody glanced at her or spoke to her as she went out of her room and through the Great Hall, passed the kitchen and continued down the stairs. It was very dark, but she found her way by touch.

When she reached the bottom of the stairs, her groping hand found the rough wood of the cellar door. She turned the handle and went in.

Grace had expected the cellar to be in complete darkness, the way it had been on that terrible night; but there was a very faint glimmer of light. Grace stopped, her hand still on the door, her eyes widening as she tried to make out what was causing that ghostly glow. It seemed to be coming from the end wall of the cellar, the ancient wall of rough stones, and for a moment Grace could not think what it was.

Then a dark shadow moved across the light. Grace gave a start of fear. Now she understood: there was already a gap in the stones, and the moonlight was shining through.

The movement came again. It was a shadow — the shadow of a man; and the moonlight sparked a flash of silver from something in his hand. Grace caught her breath, and almost bit through her lip. It was the shadow of a man holding a knife.

Then the shadow moved again, and a whisper came to her ears. It was so low that she could almost have imagined it; but she would have known that voice anywhere. To her, it was the most beloved sound on earth.

'Grace,' whispered Enda. 'Is that you, Grace?'

She moved forward confidently, guided by the moonlight. Enda held out his hand, and Grace reached out her own to meet it; and then his arms were around her, holding her tightly to him.

'I heard you were back,' was all he said, but it was enough.

After a moment, Enda let Grace go and stepped out through the hole he had made in the wall.

'Wait a minute,' Grace whispered. In that instant, when his arms had been around her, she had remembered that night in Queen Elizabeth's court when, wearing her gold necklace and dressed in silk and velvet, she had whirled around to the sound of violins. For her, she knew, all that was over forever; and she did not care.

She took the gold necklace from around her neck and placed it gently back in the crevice where she had found it. Perhaps someone in the future, someone whose need was desperate, would find it. Grace would not need jewellery and fine clothes any more. Her future was with Enda.

She stepped through the hole and waited while Enda replaced the stones. Then, putting her hand in Enda's, she jumped down into the ditch.

The soldiers had arrived at the gate on the castle's eastern side. Grace could hear the officer calling out to the defenders to give up Don Octavio, and the sound of shots by way of reply. Under cover of the noise, Grace and Enda could make their way safely down the west side. Cautiously, keeping in the shadow of the hedge, they slipped down to the lane and across the Rough Field.

As they went, Grace realised that she was not afraid as she had been on that night in November. Her heart was not beating wildly, her forehead was not sticky with sweat, and her hands were steady. Too much had happened to her.

'I will never be frightened again,' she said, 'and I will never cry again.'

She said the words aloud, but she knew that Enda could scarcely hear her voice through the musket-fire and the ominous booming of the cannon.

When they reached the little cottage by Lough Fergus, the door stood wide open. In a moment Grace, still keeping hold of Enda's hand, was in Bridget's arms.

There was another explosion, the sound of the cannon once more cutting through the air; but this time there were no musket-shots in answer. There was a deafening grinding and rumbling sound, and then one final explosion, as huge stones which had not moved for hundreds of years went crashing to the ground. The great grey castle of Drumshee was gone.

CHAPTER SIXTEEN

'So you are determined to marry him, my dear?' Brendan Davoren's face was worried.

'Yes,' said Grace. She said no more, but her voice was clear and firm.

Brendan smiled. 'Well,' he said resignedly, 'I suppose you're sixteen now and you'll have to have your own way. You won't have too much to live on, I'm afraid. I've talked to the Queen again and again, but she maintains that the estate of Drumshee must be confiscated by the Crown because it sheltered one of Her Majesty's enemies. Out of the mercy of her heart — those are her words — she'll allow you to keep a hundred acres out of your four thousand.'

'A hundred acres!' Grace jumped to her feet and ran across to the door of the cottage. 'Enda, we'll have a hundred acres! We can get married on that!'

Enda was in the yard, grooming Golden Dawn, while Bridget fed the hens nearby. She looked up with a smile, and Enda came over to the door with a flush on his smooth brown cheeks. He looked at Brendan in an embarrassed way, and Brendan clapped him on the shoulder.

'You might as well give in, my lad,' he said. 'She's a very determined little lady. You'll be able to manage on a hundred acres?'

Enda looked at him with a smile.

'Grace doesn't need any acres,' he said. 'We'd be happy with just my farm. But with a hundred acres, we'll be rich as well as happy.'

Grace smiled. Brendan had given his consent, and that was all that mattered. He was her sole guardian — he had been ever since that night in September 1588, when the Fitzgeralds and Don Octavio had refused to join their servants in surrendering to the soldiers, and had been killed when the castle collapsed.

All through April and May, Enda — with help from Joe and Tom and many other friends and neighbours — built a new house at Drumshee. He did not build it exactly where Drumshee Castle had stood — the new house was outside the old enclosure, on the hill's south slope, where it would be sheltered from the strong west winds — but he used many stones from the old castle.

The house was a small one. It had a big kitchen, with an iron crane over the fireplace to hold the pots, and on either side of the kitchen was a bedroom; and above these three rooms was a big loft. The loft was a good place for storage, and the first thing that was put there was the sandalwood chest, sealed with wax, which the captain of the *Seagull* had brought over to Drumshee. When the house was finished, Enda built a cabin for the cows and a stable for the three horses — the carthorse, Golden Dawn and Golden Noon.

'I don't think I've ever seen such a beautiful house,' Grace told Enda, the day before they were married. Hand in hand, they wandered through its three rooms, which gleamed white with fresh limewash.

'It's much more beautiful than the castle was,' she added, looking at the fire burning brightly in the hearth and the two big chairs which stood on either side of the fireplace.

'It's a bit smaller,' said Enda, with a grin. 'Still,' he added, 'it's a lot warmer.'

On her wedding day, Grace opened the sandal-wood chest, took out her dress with the farthingale of rose velvet, and put it on for the first time since the night when she had been presented to the Queen. Brendan and Judith and her husband had come over for the wedding, and Judith dressed Grace's hair in the latest fashion from the court: curls piled upon curls, all held in place by a little crown of pale pink rosebuds stitched to a green velvet ribbon.

It was a beautiful morning as Grace and Enda walked down the dusty road to the little church. The hedges were pink and yellow with wild roses and woodbine, and the ditches foamed with meadow-sweet. Behind them walked all their friends and neighbours, and jokes and laughter rang out so loudly that the cows in the fields stopped munching the grass and came to the hedges to see what was happening.

Side by side, Grace and Enda knelt in front of the altar and were blessed by the kindly old priest. Then, hand in hand, they walked back from the church, wordless but happy.

When they got back to their house, they found a magnificent feast laid out. Big tables had been made out of lengths of wood placed on top of huge blocks of stone from the castle ruins. These tables were spread with linen cloths — one of the many presents Judith had brought — and down the centre of each table were bunches of roses, Grace's favourite flower, and long trails of dark green ivy.

Never had the people of the parish seen as much

food as there was at the wedding breakfast for Grace and Enda McMahon. Bridget and Deirdre had spent a week cooking, and Brendan had spent the day before in Galway city, buying everything he could possibly think of.

There were pies and salmon and trout, and cakes and cherries and strawberries, and great bowls of cream, and dainty baskets filled with sweetmeats. In fact, there was so much food that they could not find enough plates; Bridget had had to rush out to the cabbage garden and pick twenty large cabbage leaves to use as plates. Both Enda and Grace thought the cabbage leaves looked far prettier than plates, their dark forest-green showing up the bright colours of the food, but Judith looked a little shocked. None of the other guests minded, however. They were far too busy eating.

The summer before, Bridget had spent weeks making wine, and now it was all ready to drink. There was cowslip wine, lemon-balm wine, and rose-coloured mayblossom wine — but best of all was the sparkling elderflower wine, perfumed with the smell of summer itself. Enda and Grace shared a stool at the top of the table and drank each other's health in sweet golden wine. Behind them, against the trunk of a large oak tree, Judith had placed a large heart which she had made from willow wands, padded with thick emerald-green moss and starred with a hundred rosebuds.

'It's so beautiful,' said Grace. 'I wish I could keep it forever!'

'We'll remember it forever,' said Enda. 'That will be just as good.'

And so Enda and Grace were married and began their life together. Enda fed and cared for the animals — they had thirty cattle, a pig, and hens and ducks and geese — and dug the vegetable garden. Grace milked the cows and collected the eggs, and grew herbs and baked bread and made wines. They were not rich, but they were busy and healthy and very happy.

As the years went by, they had seven children. Cecilia was the first; she was Judith's goddaughter, and as prim and as pretty as her rich godmother in England. Then came Maeve, who was the clever one, always studying; and then there were four boys, Brendan, Conor, Declan and Niall, each one of them as gentle and hardworking as Enda. Last of all came Bridget. She was named after Enda's mother, of course, and she was as warm and loving as her grandmother had been. The people of the country-side were all a little shocked at Bridget, who wore boys' clothes and tried to do everything that her brothers did; but Grace only laughed and kissed her daughter's pink cheeks. Let her be happy and free here, she thought. No Queen of England will ever be able to sneer at her for being 'a wild little Irish rose'.

Each year Golden Dawn and Golden Noon had a foal, and as the children grew up each one of them had a pony of his or her own. There was Golden Lady, Golden Apple, Golden Sun, Golden Moon and Golden Star, Golden Boy and Golden Girl. And the McMahon children rode the green hills, and jumped the rivers and the streams, and listened to the song of the skylark, and were as happy as the day is long.